HISTORY AND TORAH

HISTORY
AND
TORAH

ESSAYS ON JEWISH LEARNING

JACOB NEUSNER

Assistant Professor of Religion
Dartmouth College
Hanover, New Hampshire

SCHOCKEN BOOKS · NEW YORK

Printed in Great Britain

CONTENTS

TO MY FATHER-IN-LAW
MAX RICHTER
Exodus 18.24

INTRODUCTION

THESE ESSAYS CONTAIN a statement of elements of Jewish faith as understood by a Jewish historian. With notable exceptions, historians in the recent past have refused to admit that they study for other than strictly historical motives. However, one may engage in research with objectivity, and yet affirm that the choice of subject and degree of passion in pursuing it emerge from one's own situation. My choice of subject and interest in it are the consequence of my situation as a Jew, which I therefore begin by describing.

The Jewish situation endows me, first of all, with a long and formidable perspective. It forces me to see myself as part of a continuum of time and of space, as heir of some of the most sublime and most foolish men that have ever lived, and as friend and brother of men who, in days past, lived almost everywhere men have been. I cannot therefore accept provinciality, either temporal or spatial, or see myself as rooted forever in one culture or in one age.

Thus the Jewish situation is international and cosmopolitan, and never wholly part of one place or time. This is both a blessing and a curse. It is a blessing because it assures me of ultimate detachment, of a capacity to contemplate from without, to think less fettered by rooted attachments than other men. It forces not only detachment, but to some measure, an act of selection and judgment also, for, not being fully committed anywhere or ever, I am forced to perceive what other men may stand too close to see, and in perception, to respond, to judge. I must therefore learn to love with open arms, to know that this land, this people are mine, yet not wholly so, for I belong to Another as well. Thus to be a Jew means in a historical and more than historical sense to be always homeless in space and in time,

7

always aware of the precariousness of security, of the possibility, by no means remote, that I may have to find another place.

But the Jewish situation of homelessness, of detachment, has provided me, secondly, with the awareness that what is now is not necessarily what was, nor what must always be. Being able to stand apart because of an inherited and acquired perspective of distance, I realize that men have choices they may not themselves perceive, that there have been and are now other ways of conducting life and living with men, of building society and creating culture, than those we think are normative. Being able to criticize from the perspective of other ages and lands, I am enabled to evaluate what others may take for granted, to see the given as something to be criticized and elevated.

Third, the Jewish situation of living with a long perspective imposes upon me a terrible need to find something meaningful, truly eternal in human affairs. If I see that all things change, and that only change is permanent, then I need all the more a sense of what abides in man, of what endures in human civilization. If one says, with Sinclair Lewis' men of Gopher Prairie, that to build the emporium that is ours, Washington weathered the rigours of Valley Forge, Caesar crossed the Rubicon, and Henry stood at Agincourt, then one declares his faith that what is here is truly the Zenith and the end of Western history. But we Jews know differently, for we know of cities once great and now no more, of civilizations—and we too have built civilizations—that prospered and were wiped out in time. We ask, therefore, because we need to ask: what abides, what is permanently meaningful in life? We want to know where history is moving, because we know that history does, indeed, move.

Fourth, out of this need, this thirst for meaning in kaleidoscopic life, we Jews have learned that something in man is indeed eternal. We use the words of Scripture, and say that man is 'made in the image of God', but underlying

8

these words is a mute and unarticulated awareness that man prevails, and some of his achievements can endure. We know, moreover, what will live, namely, the intellect, the capacity of man to learn. We have, therefore, dedicated our best energies to the cultivation of the mind, to study, enrichment, and transmission of man's insights and ideas through the ages. We have held that that part of man which may think, know, believe, hope, love—that part is divine and endures, and whatever part of it endures from another age is ours to know, love and cherish. Therefore, in other ages, our monuments have been books, the school house, and our heroes have been men of learning and of mind.

Fifth, because I am a Jew, I understand how important to the world are compassion, and man's capacity to transcend his animal base through acts of love and fellowship. The Jewish situation imposes this understanding in two ways. First, because we were slaves in Egypt, we know how important is an act freely done, freely given, that at its most elevated is represented by compassion. Because we have suffered in history, we have learned how important is the opposite of cruelty and oppression, namely, kindness and love. Second, because we see ourselves as men, neither animals nor God, neither wholly objects of nature and history nor wholly subjects of nature and history, we see our human duties and capacities as neither wholly passive nor on the other hand entirely active. We know, therefore, that men may *do* little, but that he may *do*: and what he may do as an act of his own will is to act decently, compassionately, justly, for his free will permits him to choose compassion. The larger part of his life may be 'conditioned', and outside of his power, but that precious corner of freedom to act by one's own will remains, and *will* at its most virtuous is goodwill, in Hebrew *hesed* (in the abstract, compassion) and *gemilut hasadim* (in the concrete, acts of compassion).

Sixth, more concretely, the Jewish situation imposes upon me an intensity of human relationship, best embodied in

9

the family and people, that others see as clannishness. Seeing the world as we do, a lonely, insecure, transitory place, we look within it for places of security and evidences of permanence, and these we find, as I said, in the abstract in compassion, and in the concrete, in human relationships of love and deep acceptance. We know that death is always near, and that each man goes his separate way to death. But we find in this knowledge not only separateness, but also union of the generations. Death is the experience that brings together the generations that have gone before and those that will come; it is the one experience we share in common, and the Jewish forms of death—the sanctification of God's name on this one stark moment when we are forced to recognize His power and His will—abide to unite the generations. This is the source of veneration of our past, and our capacity continually to live in it, and the foundation of our love for our people, wherever and whenever they are found.

Finally, the Jewish situation has at its foundation a continuing confrontation with the reality of God. Until now, one may have wondered where is the 'theology' of the Jewish situation. Beyond the theologies of Jewish religion, and before them all, is the simple sentence, 'In the beginning God created the heaven and the earth.' That is our fundamental affirmation, and all else must be built on that fact. We affirm that God, who made the world, did so purposefully, and ultimately that purpose is revealed in the course of human history. All that I have said about our long and formidable perspective, our awareness of the frailty and transitory quality of man, our thirst for permanence, through dedication to the mind and reason, to love and compassion, in the abstract and in concrete terms—all this is founded upon our fundamental attitude toward the world and ourselves, both of which we see to be the objects of divine concern, divine purpose, divine compassion. Both men and nature are objects, not subjects, of reality, both are profane, and the only sanctity lies beyond the world and man.

Hence our concern for history and its movement, for man and his conduct in society arises out of our awareness that in the objects of creation we see in pale reflection a shadow of the Subject.

Because of this awareness, we are not ashamed of our history, of our frailty and inconsequentiality as a small and insignificant people among the peoples of mankind. We know that those great nations that ruled the world like God perished like men, while we who have patiently endured in hope endure today. Therefore we do not reject our tragic past.

Very little has been said here to distinguish Jews from other men. It is hardly necessary to be a Jew to understand the Jewish situation. The existential qualities I have described are those that Jews may know best and longest, but that others know too. We have words for our situation, such as *Galut*, exile, *Rachmanut*, compassion, *Yosher*, righteousness, and *Bitahon*, faith, trust in God; and these words, though ultimately not translatable into any other language, are in fact shared existentially by every other people today.

In a sense, therefore, just as, on account of Hiroshima, we are all murderers, so, on account of Auschwitz, we are all Jews. Just as we men incinerated entire cities in our fury, so we men were incinerated, shot, gassed, starved, destroyed in our frailty. An age that is threatened by the total destruction of entire civilizations knows what it means to be Jews, who suffered the destruction of their entire European civilization in our time. An age that knows no security knows what it means to be Jews, who have lived for thousands of years without security. An age that finds itself almost powerless to change the course of history, in which individuals find they are almost impotent to affect events, knows what it means to be Jews, who have lived as outsiders, standing always on the wings of history and never in the spotlight. An age that suddenly realizes it is in the grip of past events, knows what it means to be Jews, who have seen themselves forever in the grip of events they have not caused, and ultimately, in the hand of a Providence. An age that now knows the danger of nationalism and provinciality knows what it means to be Jews, who have lived internationally before there were nations.

If this is so, perhaps others will learn from us the affirmative lessons of our situation: our quest for meaning in events, our consecration to the human intellect and capacity to think, to create and preserve culture; our appreciation of the preciousness and sanctity of man's slender treasure of compassion and of love, in the abstract and also in day-to-day human relations in which, after all, we do retain considerable power; and, finally, our awareness of the reality, immediacy, and centrality of God's will, our knowledge that in the end, it is not we but God who determines the history of men and nations, not we but God with whom men must strive for blessing.

For me Judaism can mean only classical Judaism, in which I discern four dominant motifs: belief in the Creator of man and nature and in the need to acknowledge gratefully the artifacts of his sovereignty; belief in relevation and acceptance of the abiding authority of revealed law; belief in the centrality of study of the Torah in the religious life; and belief in the ultimate coming of the Messiah.

The essays that follow focus on the third of these themes, the requirement imposed by Judaism of continuing study of the Torah as the central discipline in life, as the act which man was created to do. The first group of papers is concerned with the relationship between revelation and history, between eternal truth and an inconstant world. Jews have doggedly insisted that they preserve the faith as of old, and have found it possible to engage in study of the Torah (or, in the current phrase, in Jewish learning) precisely on account of that insistence. The Torah demands man's attention because it contains the revealed faith. At the same time Jews have found it possible to read into the authoritative texts of the past their most current perplexities. As a historian, I affirm that what has gone before, even in the remote past, remains interesting and in a measure paradigmatic for the new age. In 'History and Midrash' I have tried to explain the process by which time-bound Scriptures have been rendered eternally contemporary, while in 'Intellectual Honesty in Jewish Learning' are pointed out some of the dangers of this process. My conviction is that in the end, we shall *believe* only what we *know* to be true, and that knowledge and our certainty of its truth rest upon precise mastery of the ancient sources and rational inquiry into their significance, whether that be historical, theological, or legal. That rational inquiry cannot, however, follow canons of thought different from those which govern our thinking about other aspects of reality, and the results of that inquiry must likewise emerge as congruent to the other ideas which occupy our minds. In 'The Eighty-Ninth Psalm: Paradigm of Israel's Faith', I have tried to demonstrate with one text how a discrete document may, within broad limits, be made to yield a comprehensive statement of classical Judaism. This is, quite obviously, a midrashic approach in the sense defined in the first paper, but I believe a self-evidently valid one.

The second and third groups of papers deal with the theory and practice of Jewish learning, respectively. In 'City, Society, and Self: Goals for Jewish Learning' and 'Scholars and Machines', I have tried to show how study of the Torah may have moral value, and how the existential attitudes embodied in traditional Jewish approaches to intellectualism may illuminate current perplexities in other intellectual enterprises. The social and historical importance to Diaspora-Jewry of Jewish learning is described in 'Motivations for Jewish Learning in the Golah.' I share the conviction of Jews of former generations that the Jews are not 'just like everybody else', and that the meaning of being a Jew rests upon the unique situation of the Jewish people in history. What has always set the Jew apart is his dedication to study and fulfilment of God's Torah. What is unique in contemporary Jewry, from the perspective of Jewish history, is its indifference to study of the Torah and fulfilment of the commandments.

The ancient Jewish thirst for learning is quenched by contemporary Jews at other waters, and the 'waters of life' are not even tasted by most of them. For many, the purpose of learning is ultimately worldly profit, and thus we find ourselves possessed of full bellies and empty heads. Golah-Jewry of our day has already demonstrated that it cannot endure outside of the Torah any more than a fish can live outside of water, while past generations have given equally impressive evidence that Golah-Jewry may flourish for endless generations on the nourishment of Torah and through the nurture of its sons and daughters in Torah.

The final two papers describe the worldly consequences of dedication to Jewish learning in the lives of two diverse and interesting men. They are offered as evidence to a doubting generation in behalf of the claim that Jewish learning may meaningfully engage worldly and able people who are swept up in the tides of commonplace affairs. Rabbi Tarfon was an impulsive man of action, whose responsibility included the government of a difficult people in a trying time. Rabbi Ishmael the son of Rabbi Yosi, on the other hand, was an aristocrat in the Tannaitic age, for he was the last in a family of masters of the Torah, and saw himself as the heir of vast riches, and as the final link in a chain of intellectual achievement. Unlike Rabbi Tarfon, he aspired less to acquire worldly power, though he exercised it, than to preserve and to enhance his ancient patrimony. In modern times, Rabbi Tarfon might be most at home in a legislature or market-place, while Rabbi Ishmael might have found himself at ease in benign retirement. In their own day, both men found a place for themselves in the Tannaitic academies. Rabbi Tarfon shows how learning and deeds may provide reciprocally and in equal measure the substance for a vigorous life, while Rabbi Ishmael the son of Rabbi Yosi demonstrates how in intellectual affairs one may properly conduct himself as heir of the wealth and splendour of former generations.

These papers were originally printed as follows: 'History and Midrash', *Judaism* IX, i, 1960; 'Intellectual Honesty', *The Reconstructionist*, January, 1963; 'The Eighty-Ninth Psalm', *Judaism*, VIII, 3, 1959; 'City, Society, and Self', *Religious Education*, September, 1962, and *The Journal of the Central Conference of American Rabbis*, April, 1962; 'Motivations for Jewish Learning in the Diaspora' appeared as 'Why Hebrew Culture' in *The Reconstructionist*, June, 1963; 'Scholars and Machines', *Christian Scholar* XLIII, 1960; 'Rabbi Tarfon' and 'Rabbi Ishmael the son of Rabbi Yosi' in *Judaica*, XVII, 3, 1961, and XVI, 1, 1960, respectively.

These essays find unity in my conviction that Judaism preserves within itself the power to engage both mind and heart, and the immediate relevance to render such engagement consequential for both society and the individual. Each Jew is bound to study the Torah, and to respond to what he learns in a personally significant manner. Normative response takes the forms of ethical action and religious observance. The enterprise of the Jewish mind may, even within its own terms, provide the substance for a rich and worthy intellectual life. This proposition provides the basis for each paper, and serves to draw all together into a statement on the meaning of Jewish learning in the present age.

My thanks are due to Rabbi Jack Riemer for numerous sage comments, and to the following, with the help of whose generous grants this book was published: Dartmouth College, and, in particular, the Committee on Research of Dartmouth College; the Torah Fund of Rabbi Dudley Weinberg, Temple Emanuel-Bne Jeshurun of Milwaukee, Wisconsin; The National Foundation for Jewish Culture, and in particular Dr. Judah J. Shapiro, its secretary.

JACOB NEUSNER.

Hanover, New Hampshire, U.S.A.
Erev Rosh Hodesh Elul 5724
August 7, 1964.

I

HISTORY AND MIDRASH

'There is no hope in returning to a traditional faith after it has once been abandoned, since the essential condition in the holder of a traditional faith is that he should not know he is a traditionalist . . .'
Al Ghazali

HOLY SCRIPTURE POSED to the sages of the Talmudic epoch a more perplexing problem than simply to uncover the plain meaning of the sacred words. Their problem, which still troubles text-centred religions, was how to discover in ancient writings continuing truths and meaning for a very different time. Their answer to this problem was *Midrash*, the exegesis and exposition of revealed Scripture. In truth, Scriptural interpretation was as old as Scripture, and elements of *Midrash* are present in the Hebrew Bible itself. The particular achievement of the sages was to explore the implications of *Midrash* and to exploit its formidable techniques in the cause of a sophisticated and highly contemporary religion.

The rabbis found that they had to expound the religion of a text ascribed to Moses, who had preceded them by more than a millennium, to congregations in the first centuries of the common era. They had to make sense out of the great teachings of the past, and to apply them to the present situation. Far more than this, however, they had to come to grips with the *realia* of the Scripture that conveyed these truths. The sages were concerned not only with the content, but with the very context of revelation. Their inheritance was a record of revelation whose minutest detail demanded assent from the pious man. If these ancient words were to bear truth for all time, they had to make good sense always and everywhere. The rabbis would not, therefore, pass silently over some bothersome detail which did not harmonize with their idea of truth or good manners. They would not deny the Bible's claim to detailed authenticity. 'If it is empty—from you,' that is, if you find no meaning in a verse, the fault is yours. Scripture could not be reduced to an essence; every word was somehow essential.

Confronted with some Biblical incident which did not accord with proper morals, the rabbis could not dismiss the matter as inconsequential. At the same time, they could not justify an ethical outrage by pointing out the primitive standards of an ancient generation. If, like modern critics, they were to explain some improper action as evidence of the antiquity of a given passage, they would thereby have confessed that Scripture bore relevance to the archaeologist or historian of religion, but by no means offered appropriate instruction for a more advanced age. The rabbis would not claim that the more detailed precepts of Scriptures were addressed to one particular generation except where the Bible itself makes this clear. They would not admit that its truth was relative, appropriate only to an early and savage time. To them the truth of the Bible was eternal, standing as an imperative to man.

This problem continues to perplex men. The Bible speaks to a primitive and naïve universe. Has the passage of time muted its voice? Liberals in days past used to say that the Bible is not a text book for natural science. But liberals did not believe in revelation. Fundamentalists offered ingenious explanations for the real intent of Scripture; for example, the seven days of Creation represent seven aeons of time.

But the Bible does not say so. Must a man share the Biblical viewpoint on theology, cosmology, anthropology, in order to hold on to its ultimate consequence of faith in God and in the message of religion? History forced upon the sages a search for harmony between the detailed text and the contemporary view of metaphysics and man. This search was not the consequence of negation but of affirmation. Few men today take the Biblical claim with sufficient earnestness to continue that search.

In the *Midrash*, the rabbis were not intentionally traditional. They did not wonder how to save a text they might already have come to doubt, nor did they set out in order to sustain Scripture as a possibility for their piety. For the sages, Torah had made manifest the emergent truth that underlies all things. It was the divine design for the universe. To contrive to demonstrate harmony between current truth and Torah would be to reveal the obvious. Revelation was eternal and always in harmony with new visions of the truth. If the rabbis were traditionalists, they never knew it.

The Bible itself made possible Midrashic elucidation. The very first word of God was light. The *Talmud* says, " Is not my word like fire, saith the Lord, and like a hammer which breaks the rock into pieces?' (Jeremiah 23:29). Just as a hammer strikes the anvil and kindles clouds of sparks, so does Scripture yield many meanings, as it is said, 'Once did God speak, but two things have I heard . . .' (Psalm 62:11)". The rabbis assumed that Torah was the indivisible, exhaustive account of the event of revelation at Sinai. It revealed some truth, and encompassed all truth. Hence it was their task to draw out of the given text the widest possible range of religious insight. They did not need to distinguish between the obvious sense of words and the subtler secondary meanings words might hide. Plain sense (*p'shat*) is simply what was immediately apparent. *Midrash* was the level of meaning discovered by search (*d'rash*), by disciplined and careful exegesis. The truth was one, but the rabbis came upon the part uncovered by *Midrash* with a little more effort. (It is true that the rabbis did distinguish occasionally between a particularly imaginative *Midrash* of a verse and its plain-sense, but this distinction meant far less to them than it does nowadays.)

A classic exposition of the nature of *Midrash* is Professor Shalom Spiegel's introduction to 'Legends of the Bible' by Louis Ginzberg, in which he writes:

'Just as a pearl results from a stimulus in the shell of a mollusk, so also a legend may arise from an irritant in Scripture. The legend of Cain and Lamech has its foothold in two passages of Scripture. One passage tells of a sign granted by Cain as a warning to all who might threaten his life: anyone that slays Cain shall suffer sevenfold vengeance (Genesis 4:15). The other is the address of Lamech to his wives, reckless with swagger or savagery: I kill a man for just wounding me! (Genesis 4:25).

'This is a brutal and bad boast in a book such as the Bible, but in reality it is less bothersome than the earlier statement in Genesis 4:15 . . . After all, the bluster of a braggart or bully need not be believed literally . . . Genesis 4:15 cannot be so lightly dismissed . . . The pledge given to Cain presupposes a peculiarly ferocious form of blood-feud: any attack on the bearer of the sign is to be avenged by the slaughter of seven members of the tribe to which the assailant belonged. The archaeologist might conclude . . . that some of the stories in the book of Genesis preserve exceedingly ancient traditions . . . often antedating by centuries the birth of Biblical religion . . . But in all times men have turned to the Bible not only for antiquarian curiosities, but for spiritual uplift and guidance. To such readers it must be distressing . . . to find the Holy Writ ascribing to the Deity itself the acceptance without protest of an institution of primitive law . . . Many will prefer to believe that this cannot be the meaning of the sacred writings . . .

'When facts or texts become unacceptable, fiction or

legend weaves the garland of nobler fancy. This is how the story of Cain's slaying was born . . .

'The tale runs: Lamech was a burly but blind giant who loved to follow the chase under the guidance of his son, Tubal-Cain. Whenever the horn of a beast came in sight, the boy would tell his father to shoot at it with bow and arrow. One day he saw a horn move between two hills; he turned Lamech's arrow upon it. The aim was good, the quarry dropped to the ground. When they came close to the victim, the lad exclaimed: "Father, thou hast killed something that resembles a human being in all respects, except it carries a horn on its forehead!" Lamech knew at once what had happened: he had killed his ancestor Cain, who had been marked by God with a horn for his own protection, "lest anyone who came upon him should kill him" (Genesis 4:15). In bitter remorse Lamech wept: 'I killed a man to my wounding!' (Genesis 4:24).

'. . . What seemed to be shocking Scripture was made by this legend to yield a moral tale. Genesis 4:24 was turned from a barbarian boast into a cry of contrition: The offensive "I kill a man for just wounding me" was not read "I killed a man to my wounding and sorrow." The Hebrew permits this change by a mere inflection of voice. But above all, the stumbling block in Genesis 4:15 was removed: the assurance of the deity that Cain's vengeance shall be sevenfold was made to mean that his punishment will be exacted from him in the seventh generation. His sentence was to be carried out by Lamech, the seventh in the succession of generations since Adam. The savage reprisal . . . became a deserved but deferred penalty, the merciful Judge, slow to anger, granting the sinner a long reprieve to repent and mend his ways. In brief, two passages of the sacred Writ, disturbing the peace and disquieting the faith of a host of pious readers in every age, were metamorphosed in this legend of Cain and Lamech to yield the edifying lesson: even the arrow of a sightless archer obeys the holy will and word of God.

'. . . Any vestige of reprehensible or primitive practices was read away, and Scripture brought to conform to the advanced conscience of a later state in civilization.'

A second type of *Midrash* was inquiry into the legal portions of the Pentateuch to discover laws to apply to a new situation, or to uncover Scriptural basis for an apparent innovation in law. An example of such legal *Midrash* was the effort to demonstrate the real meaning of 'an eye for an eye'. The sages held that the verse clearly means that one should exact the monetary equivalent of an eye for the loss of an eye, and no more. One proof, among many brought by Talmud, is derived from Numbers 35:31, 'Thou shalt not take ransom for the life of a murderer . . .' This means, 'for the life of a murderer thou shalt not take ransom, but thou shalt take ransom for limbs.' Scripture thus means, and has always meant, that a ransom may compensate loss of a major limb.

Midrash represents, therefore, creative philology and creative historiography (in the phrases of Professor Y. Heinemann in '*Darchei Ha-Agadah*'). As creative philology, the *Midrash* discovers meaning in apparently meaningless detail. It creates out of the fabric of silence as of speech. Even parts of speech are set out, each by itself, each hiding its special message for some perplexity. As Dr. Max Kadushin demonstrated in 'The Rabbinic Mind', the *Midrash* uses the elements of language not as fixed, unchanging categories, but as relative, living, tentative nuances of thought. As creative historiography, the *Midrash* rewrites the past to make manifest the eternal rightness of Scriptural paradigms. What would it be like if all men lived at one moment? This the *Midrash* sets out to reveal, justifying David by the criteria of Stoic philosophy and even by Roman imperial law, and thundering pious curses at the heads of men behaving in accord with the morality of their own age. *Midrash* thus exchanges the stability of language and the continuity of history for stability of values and the eternity of truth.

In the Bible, the rabbis treasured a many-splendoured jewel, now to be admired in one light, now in another. Each word has many modulations of meaning, awaiting the sensitive touch of a troubled soul to unfold a special message for a particular moment in time. *Midrash* teaches that for all times and to all times and to all men, Scriptural values are congruous and consistent. Lamech and a man fifteen centuries later are judged by the same ethics, for Scripture and its people are wholly in harmony with the sophisticated morality of any age. History does not apply to revelation. There are no relative truths. Revelation happened under the aspect of eternity: one God, one Torah, one truth for all men in every age.

Is the technique of Midrashic thought available to bring harmony between the Word and today's world?

It might be argued that *Midrash* represents speculation in terms of the concrete on the inner nature of reality, a kind of mythopoeic technique. Dr. Henri Frankfort (in 'Before Philosophy') said of myth that its imagery 'is nothing less than a carefully chosen cloak for abstract thought. It represents the form in which experience becomes conscious.' The Stoic interpreted Homer as allegory, and so made him make sense to their age. If faith speaks out in concrete images, ought Scripture to be understood as the embodiment of cosmic truth in earthly garments? Other men have tried this way before, and come to viable faith. Is this way still open? It is, and it is not.

In a rigorous sense, the techniques of *Midrash* are unavailable because men have ceased to think only in concrete images. Mythopoeic thought never leaves the concrete, and its concepts exist only in their particular forms. Death does not happen, it is. Yet abstraction is the very soul of the modern intellect. Moreover, men no longer see abstractions in the supple fabric of immediate situations. The rabbis did, using language here in one sense, there in another. The very creative force of *Midrash* depends on such stubborn particularization. For *Midrash*, language is finite, its meanings are emergent, but morality is infinite. Long ago, though, men abandoned the relativity of language for the relativity of values.

Not only is the creative philology of *Midrash* unavailable, but its classic assumptions on history are no longer widely held. Men cannot always come both to perceive the historical setting of Scripture and to assent to its moral rightness. Lamech may teach an ethical truth, but not in the first place. The courts of Israel might always have enforced a merciful form of the *lex talionis*, but Scripture does not say so openly. The *Midrash* denies relativity between history and morality. Yet if a man today recognizes the primitive in art and literature, he surely cannot refuse to see it in religion and ethics. To the rabbis, creative historiography meant that whatever was discovered in Scripture was the plain-sense from Sinai. They did not mobilize their formidable power of inventiveness and fantasy in order to avoid an apparent heresy. Scripture makes sense, and *Midrash* merely uncovers it. But if a man today makes the effort to uncover hidden truths and distant meanings, this is the ratification of heresy, for he knows he is trying to restore a tradition and to sustain it.

The idea of history has supplanted the idea of an abiding plain-sense. The historian wonders, what did this text mean to its writer? *Midrash* asks what meaning is there now, and identifies this meaning with the original intent of the writer. None would claim, though, that his present knowledge of the truth is what the truth has always been. The dilemma of the American Constitution is an obvious consequence of such self-conscious historicism. On the one hand, the unity and continuity of law demand that the twentieth-century judge speak in the name of an eighteenth-century Constitution. On the other hand, the founding fathers could not even remotely have written into their Constitution the subtle intentions discovered by the judges. One result is an ingenious *Midrash* that creates 'The Constitution', a kind of Platonic ideal which is the ultimate referent of Constitutional phenomena. Another is the dogged and progressively less convincing assertion that this was the true intention of the Convention of 1787, or would have been if they were here. A less appropriate case shows what happens when people think that the truth as it is now perceived is what it always was. The article on Beria in the Soviet Encyclopedia was published before his fall. In many columns of text he was extolled as a pillar of Soviet society. After he lost the struggle for succession, he was pilloried as a bestial traitor. The publishers had to supply subscribers with a long insertion to paste over the original article. To Soviet man, this insertion was the new version of the truth as it always was. It was truth discovered, not invented; genuine, not contrived history. For the Western intellect, this is whimsy. What truth there is is finite and provisional. Today, one cannot, therefore, embark on the quest for eternal contemporaneity. A self-conscious man does not see in a given text a truth that was of old, is now, and ever will be, in the sense that a historian understands these words. The truth of old was what the writer meant. The truth now cannot necessarily be what one would have had the writer mean.

The search for an eternal plain-sense for Scripture was the only way to preserve both the historicity and the viability of text-committed faith. That search has found only gall and wormwood for the literalist. Whenever he turns, he meets problems he must somehow explain away. Even if his heart is hard as granite, he must in the end suspect that the phenomena of universe, man, and the day the sun stood still are best explained not by the Bible but by the tentative suggestions of the natural and social sciences.

The recognition of *Midrash* teaches the distinction between what is history and what is homily. It raises a question to trouble modern exegetes: has Scripture yielded this meaning because this is what it has always meant in its own context? Or has this meaning come in order to make good sense out of a difficult verse?

While the techniques and assumptions of *Midrash* are

mostly obsolete, the purposes of *Midrash* are still very relevant. The perception that there is indeed a Midrashic dimension in a text points a way to bring to bear upon present perplexities even the power of a kind of creative philology and imaginative historiography. The Bible has both a plain meaning and an eternal message for all men everywhere. These two levels of meaning are not to be confused. The *Midrash* will teach how to expose the aspect of eternity and to discover the moment of truth.

Its first lesson is to distinguish between history as experienced by believing man and history as observed and elucidated by dispassionate scholarship. It opens the way to distinguish between the sacred history handed down by creed and faith, and the objective, critical history uncovered by the scholar. (Professor H. Richard Niebuhr makes this distinction in 'The Meaning of Revelation'.)

Its second lesson is, in truth, how to endow Scripture with life. This is to be done through homily, anachronism, and especially through the sensitive response of the modern student of religion. When the preacher finds rich and compelling meaning in a verse, this is the living verse. This is Scripture as men may believe in it and live by its message. The faculty of *Midrash* was not buried with the sages of the *Talmud*. It is always in the hand of the preacher who comes to create parables and homilies to explain and enhance the text. This secondary level of meaning in Scripture is its sacred history. Plain sense teaches the meaning of the Bible in its time: what the writer wrote and meant. *Midrash* teaches the meaning for any time: what He-Who-Spoke-and-Created-by-his-Word has to say. The final truth about the Bible surely lies, at the very least, in both places.

Third, *Midrash* warns scholars not to cross the unmarked frontier between history as it is lived and re-enacted today and history as it is observed. Bible critics have been tempted to impose on it elaborate and ingenious schemes of events; they have reconstructed the history of ancient Israel by blueprints borrowed from alien civilizations; they have thought to find an empty room when they penetrated into the holiest precincts of Jewish faith; they have even ignored the canons of common sense and precise knowledge in their wonderful speculations. Critical history, however, demonstrates what happened or, most certainly, what could not have happened at a given point in time. Historical material leans to the most delicate of judgements on what actually did happen; even archaeology is mostly useless without corroborating texts. The text itself conveys much more, and yet considerably less, than the facts of what occurred. In the end, however, if the setting of revelation is the concern of normative history, the fact and meaning of revelation are not. Scholars speaking *ex cathedra* need also to keep aware of the idea of *Midrash*. As men of faith they may very well offer profound insight. As scholars, they ought not to confuse the quality of two very different kinds of truth. The plain sense of an ancient text is not necessarily what makes sense today at all.

Furthermore, scholarship may not offer genuine understanding of a text, at all, at its first level of meaning. Scholars speculate, for example, on what the unknown Prophet of the Exile meant by the story of the suffering servant. Confessional history may indeed impel the Jew to see chapter 53 of Isaiah as the paradigm of Israel's history among the nations. Christians see in the chapter the prefiguration of Christ's life among men. It seems unlikely that scholars will come to determine decisively the original intent of the prophet whose name they do not know. For normative history, it would matter very much if they did. For confessional history, it would simply open the way to new *Midrash*.

Finally, the idea of *Midrash* teaches the lesson that the Bible, itself, is a kind of *Midrash*, as a confessional history of humanity. It is in the first instance an interpretation of events whose reality is perceived through the veil of time and in the shadowed light of faith. As the *Midrash* transformed the pragmatic events of Scripture into a paradigm

27

for a later age, so the Bible, and especially the Prophets, transformed the extraordinary history of Israel into a *Midrash* on life itself.

Men's awareness of history divorces *Midrash* from plain-sense. The specific techniques of the *Midrash* are mostly obsolete. Men have lost the capacity to believe that a particular sense of Scripture uncovered today was its eternally present meaning. They do not even expect to find eternal meanings. Even the critical scholarship of one generation has come to seem like *Midrash* to the next. I think, however, that we might well cling to the faith of the *Midrash*: the Bible does make some sense to every generation. We look to our ministry to teach that sense. We ought also to explore the resources of our own faith to find it, through mastering the text of the Bible and living with it day by day. Except for the literalist, however, none can look to reconcile his particular *Midrash* with the plain meaning of Scripture. Although one may recover a harmony between the text and the world, this is very far away from restoring the detailed historicity of Scripture.

The question arises whether a self-conscious, critical intellect is capable of Biblical faith, and whether such faith will generate genuine piety. The experience of the sages suggests that unencumbered inquiry into the true sense of Scripture will indeed lead to both faith and piety. Self-deception and preconceived commitments cannot. We ought, therefore, never to say, how much better were the old days than these! How much worthier was the age when men believed in mountains that skip like rams and worlds that are made in seven days, when Jews could see the plain meaning of the Song of Songs as a poem of love between God and Israel, and Christians, between God and the Church! If this is what the text described and what the tradition of Synagogue and Church expounded, then this was a faithful vision and an honest perception. All that we have, and all we shall ever have, is our own mature vision of the truth. We are left with the poignant teaching of the

Talmud: 'Rabbi Simon ben Lakish admonished, "Say not
. . . how much better were the old days than these! Say
not . . . if only Rabbi Tarfon were alive, then I should go
to study Torah with him. In the end, you only have the
sages of your own generation".'

II

INTELLECTUAL HONESTY IN JUDAISM

THE CLAIM OF Judaism on men's minds was once advanced
on the basis of truth and ultimate seriousness. Judaism
claimed to present a true and correct understanding of the
nature of the Jew, of the world, man and God. That claim
was expected to be considered seriously, and therefore to
be measured against the criteria of all that men knew, or
thought they knew, about reality. No source of insight or
information could stand apart from Judaism, and none
might be ignored.

In brief, Judaism once claimed to speak truly about God,
one and unique, who created the world and all that is, and
happens in it; who revealed His purpose and will for
creation to men through Moses and the prophets; and who
expected men to carry out that will as it was recorded in
Scripture, and elucidated by the sages of each generation.
The task of the religious Jew was to uncover, explicate, and
fulfil what was always immanent: the word of God in the
world.

If, therefore, for Philo Scripture became a mystic allegory,
or for Maimonides an Aristotelian treatise, for the Talmu-
dists a source of law, or for the Agadists a source of religious
insight, or for Rosenzweig an existential record, the reason
was always the same. The Torah could be nothing less than
the abiding source of insight and illumination, and the
alternative, that its relevance was limited by temporal or
intellectual contingency, was unthinkable.

The task of the Jew, and especially of the Jewish teacher, was to apprehend the truth of Judaism, to apply and to transmit it. The process of transmission never took precedence over the principle of truth, and it was rare that a teacher or sage, however troubled he may have been by the results of his inquiry, held back his findings or sought to distort them in order to preserve an edifice he feared might otherwise collapse. The consequence was that the tradition of Judaism was transmitted never intact but forever unimpaired.

In relatively recent times, however, some religionists, and among them Judaists, have abandoned the ultimate claim of religion, and of Judaism, to truth, in favour of lesser, tangential, or irrelevant claims. They have argued that Judaism serves noble and virtuous ends, and therefore ought to survive, or to be preserved for the next generation. For example, some argue, on behalf of religion and Judaism, that both are means to the end of a happy or well-adjusted emotional life. Therefore the psychiatrist may affirm the 'value' of religion, which, however, Freud teaches him is truly chimerical and neurotic. Judaism was born among men, however, who affirmed the reality of the unseen; who suffered deep agonies to bear the word of God; who were hardly happy or well adjusted to their age, but whose consecration to truth mattered more than good public relations, and indeed demanded of them the poorest kind of life-adjustment. Judaism moreover affirms the reality of death in the midst of life, and the mystery of suffering among men.

Some have, furthermore, come to agree that religion, and Judaism, can no longer stand before the bar of scholarship, and teach, if they do not believe, things about Scripture and about Jewish religion that they do not affirm intellectually or rationally. Hence, for example, Scriptures are treated in sermons and in the classroom as if six generations of Bible scholars have laboured in vain. The literature of the Talmudic period is taught according to historical and exegetical presuppositions that were last taken seriously (out-

31

side limited circles of halakhists) in the 18th century, and the great advances in understanding and appreciating this literature made by historians, philologists, and also philosophers are treated as profane and irrelevant, not only by Orthodox Jews. The result is that in the middle of the 20th century, after more than one hundred and fifty years of Jewish science, the *Talmud* is still taught as it was in the depths of seventeenth-century Poland, and the agonies of Krochmal or Weiss seem to have been for nothing. Furthermore, the great varieties of Judaist expression are apparently intentionally glossed over in seminary, pulpit, and schoolroom alike, and Judaism emerges as a linear, monolithic and one-dimensional enterprise that it never was originally. The apologist for Judaism must, therefore, defend a faith which emerged through a myriad of historical modulations and in a galaxy of nuances as though it was born all at once last week.

Judaism is thus represented in a guise that it never originally had, and is made to be all things to all men, but nothing in particular. It conforms to the most recent sentiment of the liberal or the conservative, depending on the circumstance, and is divested of all complexity and difficulty. A quotation from some ancient or medieval authority is sufficient to establish the authority of a given interpretation today. No wonder, then, that the specific unities of Judaism on fundamental beliefs and practices are also ignored. 'Judaism believes.' It exhibits a liberalism that borders on the latitudinarian, and yet makes demands. It has an essence, but do what you want! Everything is all right—but then, what is wrong?

If Judaism is now what we want to make of it, assumed to be true even when it is not presented in a historically sound and accurate manner, we ask ourselves why religion fears truth. Perhaps one of the most representative and sophisticated statements of the position that religion should not be taken too seriously if it is to survive was made by Friedrich Nietzsche in 'The Use and Abuse of History':

32

'A religion . . . that has to be scientifically studied throughout is destroyed at the end of it all. For the historical audit brings so much to light which is false and absurd, violent and inhuman, that the condition of pious illusion falls to pieces. And a thing can live only through a pious illusion . . . All living things need an atmosphere, a mysterious mist, around them. If that veil be taken away, and a religion, an art, or a genius condemned to revolve like a star without an atmosphere, we must not be surprised if it becomes hard and unfruitful, and soon withers. It is so with all great things "that never prosper without some illusion," as Hans Sachs says in the *Meistersinger*.'

However sound Nietzsche's criticism of certain aspects of 19th century Protestant Christianity may be, and however impressive his critique of the wedding of Christian theology and Hegelian historiography, Jews cannot affirm his general principle, that faith may live only through pious illusion. If they do, they deny their faith's most fundamental claim: to truth.

None the less, such denials are advanced by 'believing' or 'observant' Jews. They have taken three forms.

First those who want to carry out the practices of Judaism, come what may, have reduced Judaism to its practices. They state at the outset that Judaism has no theology, but only a 'theology of deeds', though occasionally they try to explicate the 'implicit theology' that they uncover in this regimen of deeds. A. J. Heschel has criticized this view trenchantly, under the name 'pan-Halakhism'. It would not be worthy of mention but for the fact that so many allegedly pious Jews hold it. It should be called what it is, namely, pious atheism, which, in the name of a this-worldly and thus finite cause, banishes God, or *tant pis*, thinking about God, from the world.

Second, among 'non-observant' Jews the view is popular that Judaism has 'no theology', and therefore we may think what we like and label it 'Judaism'. Neither integrity nor

C   33

precision applies. What one Jew says is as 'Jewish' as what another thinks, even though the first may be Moses or R. Akiba or a learned philosopher, and the other, the chief (and only) rabbi of Timbuktoo, or, *mutatis mutandis*, the president of B'nai B'rith or of a Jewish Community centre or of a synagogue. One may, however, exhibit the stigmata of prophecy or the insignia of learning, but without either the word of God or many, many years of study, one is in truth neither prophet nor sage. This view leads, moreover, to the artificial identification with Judaism of currently popular views of a given majority, and to the expression, in the name of 'Judaism', of quite secular ideas which have not yet found their way into the Jewish consensus. This view, likewise, should be characterized honestly: it is a kind of Jewish know-nothingism, and is based on ignorance more than on a humane and compassionate view emergent from Judaism itself.

Third, others, much more serious about Judaism, advance this argument: We know full well it is a lie, but we must speak and act as if it were the truth. If history contradicts theology, theology must prevail. Our task is not to transmit the faith unimpaired but intact, to pretend all things are constant in an inconstant world. These men keep all the commandments (whether they be Orthodox or Reform) but one, 'Thou shalt not bear false witness,' for they abandon the claim of Judaism in favour of its consequences. They hold, moreover, that the preservation of the institutions of Judaism and the successful management of their budgets take precedence over the purposes for which these same institutions are erected. They reject indignantly all the efforts of our forlorn philosophers to express a sound, rigorous, and coherent statement within Jewish religion, and all the findings of our historians about the origins, developments, and complexities of Judaism. The former they find wanting, the latter irrelevant. What is important is that the people believe, not whether what they believe is true. Any argument is equally valid, so long as it leads to the desired conclusion. Best of all, of course, would be no argument at all.

Judaism will survive anything but deceit. Atheism and heresy take many forms, but the most pernicious of all are the cloaks of legitimacy. The most dangerous enemies of Judaism today are therefore sentimentality and stupidity, which take the forms today of anti-intellectualism and unwillingness to reckon seriously with the scholarly endeavour and its manifold consequences.

If day by day we come to a crossroads, then the choice of the way ahead should be guided by one principle, that of undeviating loyalty to plain truth, which itself must be the consequence of integrated and fully self-conscious perceptions about the world, man, and God emergent from the living traditions of humane and scientific learning, both Jewish and Western, of yesterday and today.

'For you are my witnesses, says the Lord. When you are my witnesses, then I am the Lord, and when you are not my witnesses, then I am not the Lord.'

III

THE EIGHTY-NINTH PSALM

Paradigm of Israel's Faith

As a document of religion, Psalm 89 comprehends at once
the history and destiny of the Jewish faith. Perhaps it is not
a unity; scholars dissect the text into two or three separate
parts. In the literature of Judaism, however, the Psalm has
come down as a single statement, and in its unity, imposed
quite by accident or by intention, it presents a paradigm of
Israel's religion.

At the turning point of Israel's history, in the exile of
Babylon, the Psalmist recalls the ancient Israelite legends
of God's triumphant act of creation, His mastery of nature,
He rehearses the ancient covenant of God with Israel at
the sea, His entry into human history. He recounts the
glories of David's kingdom, and borrows from the language
of literature in David's time. He repeats the horrors of
Jerusalem's destruction, and turns finally to contemplate his
bitter grief and the grief of all whose trust is in the message
of Israel's faith. From despair he turns to the hope veiled
in the everlasting covenant.

The road from the cosmic struggle with the sea and its
monstrous children to the frail despair of Israel in *golah*
leads from Abraham, through Sinai, to the throne of David
and the sanctuary of his dynasty. Beyond the disaster of
Babylon, there appear the concepts of Torah and *mitzvot*
and the theodicy hidden in them: it is through treachery

against God and His words that Israel has come to its unhappy state. This is the twilight moment of Psalm 89, when all the past is done, and the future not yet begun. Here and now is the hour heavy with Israel's past and future history.

Verses 1–5

I will sing of the mercies of the Lord forever;
To all generations will I make known Thy
    faithfulness with my mouth.
For I have said: 'For ever is mercy built;
In the very heavens Thou dost establish Thy
    faithfulness.'
'I have made a covenant with My chosen,
I have sworn unto David My servant:
For ever will I establish thy seed,
And build up thy throne to all generations.'
                           Selah.

The overture to the Psalm presents its dominant theme: the unchanging love and faithfulness which characterize God's relationship to Israel. The Psalmist will sing forever the everlasting love of God, and proclaim His trustworthiness to all times. Out of the evidences of loyalty in the past comes surety for the future. The universe is built upon the loyalty of God, and the very heavens upon His faithfulness.

In ancient paganism, nature is charmed, it has a personality. Human society is a part of an animate, cosmic universe, and out of this universe, men borrow symbols to convey their relationship to God. These symbols are drawn from nature, from the eternal return of the seasons and of time. In Israel's religion, on the other hand, nature becomes inanimate, profane; human society is indifferent to it. Symbols drawn from the recurrent rhythm of nature are no longer relevant. Israel finds its symbols in the world of man and history of men. Dry and opaque, these symbols are social and prosaic; the relationship of God to man is

37

somehow like the relationship of man to man, contractual and precise. The universe is built on loyalty, the heavens are established on faith. The human analogue is extended outward to the universe.

Appropriately, therefore, the Psalmist opens with the total profanization of nature. All that really matters in the cosmos is the persistence of two very human characteristics.

'Thou hast said, I have made a covenant with my chosen one, and I have sworn to David my servant: "I will establish thy descendants forever, and build thy throne for all generations".' Having dismissed nature from the stage of religion, the Psalmist sets forth the symbol of the covenant, as it is especially embodied in the treaty between God and the King. He cites the prophecy of Nathan (II Samuel 7:16), 'The house is steadfast and thy kingdom will be forever before thee. Thy throne will be established to eternity.' This is the central image of God's relationship to man. Not in the eternal and recurrent rhythm of nature, but in the unique and unrepeated event of the covenant with Israel and its King do man and God meet. Out of the pragmatic relationship embodied in the ongoing history of Israel, the Psalmist discovers the paradigmatic relationship that governs forever God's deeds with men: steadfast love and loyalty to a promise. In the profane stream of time the sacred is immanent. The transcendent God who created by a word thus enters into the times of men.

These verses set out the theme of the Psalm.

Verses 6–19

So shall the heavens praise Thy wonders, O Lord,
Thy faithfulness also in the assembly of the holy ones.
For who in the skies can be compared unto the Lord,
Who among the sons of might can be likened unto
    the Lord,
A God dreaded in the council of the holy ones,
And feared of all them that are round about him?

O Lord God of hosts,
Who is a mighty one, like unto Thee, O Lord?
And thy faithfulness is round about Thee.
Thou rulest the proud swelling of the sea;
When the waves thereof arise, Thou stillest them.

Thou didst crush Rahab as one that is slain;
Thou didst scatter Thine enemies with the arm of
    Thy strength.
Thine are the heavens, Thine also the earth;
The world and the fulness thereof, Thou hast founded
    them.
The north and the south, Thou hast created them;
Tabor and Hermon rejoice in Thy name.
Thine is an arm with might;
Strong is Thy hand, and exalted is Thy right hand.

Righteousness and justice are the foundation of Thy
    throne;
Mercy and truth go before Thee.

Happy is the people that know the joyful shout;
They walk, O Lord, in the light of Thy countenance.
In Thy name do they rejoice all the day;
And through Thy righteousness are they exalted.
For Thou art the glory of their strength;
And in Thy favour our horn is exalted.
For of the Lord is our shield;
And of the Holy One of Israel is our king.

Nature, which is at once subordinate and irrelevant, plays
its role in the narration of God's might to the assembly of
His holy ones. God is utterly transcendent over nature,
which cannot even provide a proper analogy to Him. None
in nature can be compared to Him, but a quality of man
can: faithfulness.

The Psalmist recalls the ancient and pre-Mosaic Israelite

legends of God's subjugation of the sea. When God came
to make the world, He had to overcome the rebellion of
chaos and of the abyss. This is a parallel myth, embedded
in the literature of Israel, to the Babylonian *Enuma Elish*.
Marduk, god of light, defeated Tiamat, goddess of darkness,
when he made the world. Rahab is the Biblical proper
name for Tiamat and the legend appears in Isaiah, Job,
and Psalms (cf. Ps. 7:13–14, Is. 51:9, Job 7:12, 9:13, 25:12).
In this Psalm, the whole cosmos, and not only Rahab, is
subdued by God. God sweeps back the raging tempest when
the sea rises up against him (see also Psalm 93:4), and He
acquires the whole world as his private domain, even the
mountains Tabor and Hermon, which were at one time in
Canaanite history the dwellings of the gods, or even, some
speculate, their very epiphany. The Psalmist rehearses, therefore, the pre-Mosaic events in Israel's religion, and dismisses
these events and the images that embody them as inconsequential in the light of God's mighty arm and strong hand.

Rather he turns to authentic manifestations of God's
power: the human qualities of righteousness and justice.
Borrowing the symbols of human society, he cites those
qualities most crucial in relationships among men. These
very qualities are the foundations of His throne, even as
steadfast love and faithfulness minister before Him. The
people who walk in God's light see the true epiphany:
righteousness, faithful love, justice and mercy.

The very best the Psalmist can find to say for nature is
that it is all God's. When he turns to the community of
God, he finds a rich treasure of proper metaphors.

The Psalmist recalls the Song at the Sea, and actually
alludes to it (cf. Exodus 15:6, 11, 16, 17), as if to underline
his message. The true manifestations of God's power are in
the affairs of men and history. Nature is His tool, man His
prized creation.

From the revelation at the Sea, the Psalmist turns to the
sanctuary, and recalls the sound of rejoicing, the sound of
the people's shout before God and the King. (Cf. II Samuel

6:15. Numbers 23:21). In the sanctuary Israel carried on its formal and actual service to God. In the service, the covenant relationship finds substance, and the sanctuary itself witnesses to the place of the monarch, its builder, and to the symbol of the dynasty of David as bearer of the particular form of the covenant.

The Psalmist reviews, therefore, the course of divine participation in human history, from creation, to the Exodus, and finally to the sanctuary. He adumbrates the place the king has built, echoing, however, the prophetic censure of kingship, 'For our shield belongs to the Lord, even our king belongs to the Holy One of Israel.'

Verses 20–38

Then Thou spokest in vision to Thy godly ones,
And saidst: 'I have laid help upon one that is mighty;
I have exalted one chosen out of the people.
I have found David My servant;
With My holy oil have I anointed him;
With whom My hand shall be established;
Mine arm also shall strengthen him.
The enemy shall not exact from him;
Nor the son of wickedness afflict him.
I will beat to pieces his adversaries before him,
And smite them that hate him.
But My faithfulness and My mercy shall be with him;
And through My name shall his horn be exalted.
I will set his hand also on the sea,
And his right hand on the rivers.
He shall call unto Me: Thou art my Father,
My God and the rock of my salvation.
I also will appoint him first-born,
The highest of the kings of the earth.
Forever will I keep for him My mercy,
And My covenant shall stand fast with him.
His seed also will I make to endure forever,
And his throne as the days of heaven.

If his children forsake My law,
And walk not in Mine ordinances;
If they profane My statutes,
And keep not My commandments;
Then will I visit their transgression with the rod,
And their iniquity with strokes.

But My mercy will I not break off from him.
Nor will I be false to my faithfulness.
My covenant will I not profane,
Nor alter that which is gone out of My lips.
Once have I sworn by My holiness:
Surely I will not be false unto David;
His seed shall endure forever,
And his throne as the sun before Me.
It shall be established forever as the moon;
And be steadfast as the witness in the sky.

Selah.

If at the time of the sanctuary, the crucial symbol of the covenant is the monarchy, it is a symbol that imposes a painful tension. There was no king at the Sea, nor at Sinai. God Himself is the king of Israel and ruler of its destiny. If events have brought about the institution of a monarchy, this can have no role in the religion of Israel. On the other hand, events themselves retain a sanctity, and the very fact of the kingship is in some sense a manifestation of divine rule. In other ancient cultures, the king plays the role of mediator between God and the polity. He is in some places the son of God. Here is, therefore, a bitter clash of symbols, between the amphictyonic polity founded at Sinai, on the one hand, and the royal polity, on the other.

Only through the purpose of the kingdom the tension is resolved. The king finds his proper place in the religion of Israel: he is the shepherd of Israel and restores the faith of Sinai. As the messenger of God he redeems the people. The clash of image is resolved, as the Psalms and Prophets transfer the mythic, cosmological symbol of monarchy and cult into the eschatological framework of divine history. The 'circular', recurrent symbol of the king as surrogate of God is transformed into the 'linear' symbol of the redeemer who awaits to save Israel at the end of time.

In Psalm 89, the king appears as the anointed of God, as the powerful and shrewd conqueror. God's faithfulness and love, at first the foundations of the cosmos, are now the foundations of the monarchy itself. God's steadfast loyalty guarantees His covenant: to establish the royal line forever, and the throne for the days of the heavens. The passage is rich in references to David and Nathan, and has been called 'a poetical expansion of the promise to David recorded in II Samuel 7'. The titles reserved for the people Israel in Exodus 4:22 and Deuteronomy 25:19 are now applied to the king. God will punish the transgression of Israel with the rod; thus the Psalmist recalls II Samuel 7:14, and cites God's promise in I Samuel 15:29, that He will not be false, and in II Samuel 7:15, that He will not remove His love from Israel. Finally, the language of the oath central to the etiology of Jerusalem, city of David, in Genesis 14 and 15 is repeated here precisely. The language of God's promise to David concerning his son, 'I shall be a father for him and he shall be a son for Me' is repeated here, 'He will cry to me, "Thou art my Father, my God, and the Rock of my salvation." And I will make him the first-born son, the highest of the kings of the earth . . .'

In almost an off-hand aside, the Psalmist remarks that all this promise is somehow conditioned by the faithfulness of Israel. 'If his children forsake My Torah and do not walk according to My ordinances, if they violate My statutes and do not keep My commandments, then I will punish their transgression with the rod, and their iniquity with scourges, but I will not remove from him My steadfast love or be false to My faithfulness.' Here the king is seen apart from and beyond the people. Whatever the iniquity of Israel, the king will stand in the light of God, and his throne will endure through the generations of sun and moon. A king without a kingdom is a lonely figure indeed, and it is hard to understand this passage in its plain sense: whatever the people do, their monarch will reign. Over what sovereignty? The passage hints, therefore, at the messianic resolution of the royal image: the king is not really a monarch in time at all, but the sovereign who awaits the coming of his throne at the end of time.

The reference to Torah prefigures history to come. Torah vitiates the power of the royal symbolism. When Torah is actually established in the religious consciousness of Israel, the force of any other image of covenant is lost. Torah is the indwelling presence of the Divine in the life of Israel; the people keep their covenant with God by carrying out His will embodied in Torah. Even steadfast love and faithfulness are no longer necessary analogues to the divine convenant. Through Torah, God himself is present in the affairs of men. Therefore symbols borrowed from human society are no longer relevant to this relationship. With the advent of Torah, the paradigmatic events of the past, the covenant, the monarchy, are swept into the new polity and become subordinate elements in its framework. Torah embodies the new and eternally present relationship of Israel to God. In its ordinances and deeds, God is eternally present. The reference to Torah in the praises of the king is at once anachronistic and prophetic. It refers to the time past when the figure of the monarch embodied the covenant relation. It refers to the time to come when the Torah will remain the only available form of covenant left to Israel and when the monarchy will have been transformed from a reality in history into an eschatological promise. Torah does not belong alongside the monarchy, for it is the antithesis of the kingship, and its symbolism vies with that of the sovereign. The king must even copy out for himself a Torah: he is, like all Israel, subordinate to it. Israel is the dominion of God, and not of the king, 'For ye are my servants', and not the servants of servants. Having won the central role in the religion of

Israel, Torah leaves a place for the king, but out of history and beyond it. Here and now, Torah matters.

In Psalm 89, however, this has not yet come to pass. This section of the Psalm is the king's, and it only hints at the criticism of monarchy embodied in the concept of Torah. The tension of images is between the special role of the king and the place of all Israel in the covenant with God. The prophetic resolution is a messianic promise. The new embodiment of the covenant, in Torah, is a memory of the past and a promise for the future.

Verses 39–52

But Thou hast cast off and rejected,
Thou hast been wroth with Thine anointed.
Thou hast abhorred the covenant of thy servant;
Thou hast profaned his crown even to the ground.
Thou hast broken down all his fences;
Thou hast brought his strongholds to ruin.
All that pass by the way spoil him;
He is become a taunt to his neighbours.
Thou hast exalted the right hand of his adversaries;
Thou hast made all his enemies to rejoice.
Yea, Thou turnest back the edge of his sword,
And hast not made him to stand in the battle.
Thou hast made his brightness to cease,
And cast his throne down to the ground.
The days of his youth hast Thou shortened;
Thou hast covered him with shame.

Selah.

How long, O Lord? Wilt Thou hide Thyself forever?
How long shall Thy wrath burn like fire?
O remember how short my time is;
For what vanity hast Thou created all the children
of men!
What man is he that liveth and shall not see death,
That shall deliver his soul from the power of the grave?

Selah.

Where are Thy former mercies, O Lord,
Which Thou didst swear unto David in Thy
faithfulness?
Remember Lord the taunt of Thy servants;
How I do bear in my bosom the taunt of so
many peoples;
Wherewith Thine enemies have taunted, O Lord,
Wherewith they have taunted the footsteps of
Thine anointed.

The biblical narrator does not create fables. On the contrary, he tells pragmatic history, but in a paradigmatic sense. Thus the history of Israel is the Psalmist's concern, and the frame of events that gives form to that history, the relationship of God to Israel, is his framework. This is history and not myth, a story with a beginning, middle, and end. The Psalmist cannot ignore historical events. He needs to relate them to the sacralities represented by covenant, king, Torah. Only in such context, the actual history of Israel comes to enact the inner drama of human existence.

The disaster of *galut* and the consequent catastrophe for the soul of Israel are laid at God's feet. He has cast off, He has rejected, He has renounced, He has defiled the crown, He has breached the walls of the city and He has exalted the right hand of the foes. Nothing that was, happened but for Him. He is not the remote cause, but the immediate Actor. He even turned back the edge of the sword of Israel's warriors, and cut short the youth of the king. The king was crowned (II Samuel 1:10), but God cast his crown to the dust and removed the sceptre from his hand. He has impeached the man whom He consecrated, and has placed the cloak of shame on the shoulders of the people Israel.

The Psalmist identifies the story of the king and the kingdom with the story of private man. God is angry not only with the king, but with men. His wrath burns brightly against them. So the Psalmist reminds God, as it were, that

46

the life He gives is brief indeed, and that in a little while
man dies and goes down to the grave. The frailty of the
monarchy pre-figures the soul's own fragility. 'Remember
O Lord what the measure of life is, and how vain Thou
hast made mortal man.' The Psalmist closes, therefore, by
evoking the analogues of steadfast love and faithfulness.
These qualities, made manifest first in Israel's history and
then in the story of the sovereign, are evoked in the cause
of all men. 'Lord, where is Thy steadfast love of old, which
by Thy faithfulness Thou didst swear to David?' This is now
a personal and private complaint: 'Remember O Lord how
Thy servant is scorned, how I bear in my bosom the insults
of the peoples . . .' Here is an angry plea, recalling the
literature of Lamentations (Lam. 2:3 parallels vs. 44; other
parallels are in Lam. 4:20, 3:22). The pragmatic history of
the king becomes in these verses the paradigmatic history
of mortal man, 'Remember O Lord how Thy servant is
scorned . . . how they mock the footsteps of Thine anointed.'
The fate of the individual and the fate of the anointed king
have met. They are one and the same.

The past is done. Its drama is played out, and the new
act of the future has not yet begun. Yet the Psalmist raises
the curtain, revealing the slender illumination of an inex-
orable light. Faintly and dimly perceived upon the stage,
the figures of redemption, in time through Torah and
beyond it through the Messiah, wait to say their lines.

Verse 53
Blessed be the Lord for evermore.
Amen and Amen.

Ibn Ezra records that in Spain there was a wise and pious
man who found this Psalm difficult to endure. He would
not read it, and could not bear to hear it read. The Psalmist,
he said, speaks harshness and arrogance against God. Ibn
Ezra offers a stout reply: the Psalmist speaks concerning
the words of the enemies who blaspheme, recalling the

shame of God's servants, but he believes that the Messiah will come, and this is decisive.

There is another answer. Mankind cannot bear too much reality. A wise and pious man cannot well endure words which evoke the bitterness of the history and destiny of Israel. In truth, the Psalm echoes the footsteps of the Messiah, but a wise sage hears, alas, how faint and muffled they are. 'Though he tarries, yet will he come. Let me not be reminded, though, how very far away he is.'

IV

CITY, SOCIETY, SELF

Goals for Jewish Learning

As a PERSON engaged in Jewish studies and Jewish teaching, I find it relevant to ask myself how I should describe success. If my students and students everywhere engaged in the disciplines of Jewish education, were to achieve all their teachers hope for them, what, in fact, would they have accomplished, and, more important, to what end?

To reply to the question, I must attempt to describe the configuration of the ideal Jew, for to this end one educates. At the same time, I ought to describe the most desired personal consequences for Jewish education.

I should include in a description of the 'ideal Jew' elements both static and dynamic: what is he like, how does he live? The 'ideal Jew' is first of all a man who participates in the life of men, that is to say, a man of the city, neither cloistered from men nor indifferent to society. He therefore pursues an upright and honest calling, in some socially acceptable means of making a living, and need never resort to legal or moral fictions to justify his economic activity. Indeed, the meaningful and active part of his life is centred upon his calling, upon which, like other men, he lavishes his best energies; and, therefore, the elements of Judaism he inherits and embodies must be expressed within his calling and through his conduct in his calling. The first criterion, indeed, for successful Jewish education ought to be an education whose chief consequences will be manifest in the common, workaday world. Common sense demands this, for education ought to focus on the larger part of the life of man, or, ideally, on the whole man. Since the ideal Jew is first of all a man in the common society, he is likely to spend most of his life in economic endeavour, and whatever consequence his Jewish education is to have must be evident there.

The ideal Jew, as a man who participates in the life of men, must exhibit, secondly, the characteristics of fellowship. He needs to know how to live in community, and how to identify a worthy community for his efforts. I do not ignore the need merely to 'get along well with people', but that, while a social necessity, hardly exhausts the fraternal virtues. One may get on quite well with 'people' (which may mean co-workers or casual acquaintances) without in any meaningful sense *living* with them. The nexus among men is most likely to be one-dimensional and, indeed, ultimately material; one may meet the obligations imposed by such a connection without ever actually living in fellowship. Descriptively, the life of the community ought to manifest multi-dimensional kinds of relationships and connections among men, not all of them articulated or even manifested. These relationships ought to be characterized by reciprocity of profound concern, each man for the welfare and life's success of the other, each man respectful of his fellow's integrity, individuality, and uniqueness. If it is commonplace that no two men are quite alike, then it ought to be equally commonplace that every man demands a law for himself. In community, one may make connections that will bind autonomous men together, by imposing upon them, without infringing upon them, heteronomous connections defined by the need of each man to live in communion with other, different men, and the needs of a collectivity of such men to survive the individualities of its participants. The ideal Jew ought to know how to identify and participate in the community most commonly available to him, namely, the Jewish community; he may, indeed, live in several intersecting communities, formed by particularly cathectic relationships in his calling (in a university for example), or in his social, cultural, or religious life, though it is more likely nowadays that he is part of no particular community at all, if community be measured by the criteria I suggested above. In this sense, then, the ideal Jew ought to be so educated that he knows what social, communal living is, understands what it implies about the sanctity of the private person and both his autonomous and heteronomous requirements, exhibits the capacity to enter into relationships with others as singular as himself, and cherishes these relationships.

The ideal Jew, who participates in the common life and at the same time penetrates its fraternal potentialities, ought thirdly to manifest the characteristics of a developing inner consciousness. While he merges himself into the routine of the workaday world and into the web of social bonds provided by it, he ought to know how to contemplate his own uniqueness and how to develop his own singularities. If he spends most of his time with other people, none the less he is born all by himself, struggling to go back to the warmth, and he dies all by himself, a thought so pathetic and acid that by itself it may create a soul. Thus the central existential facts are as much loneliness and alienation as they are submersion and participation. The ideal Jew needs to take account of these facts, and will do so by assessing and enhancing his personal singularities by cultivating, in more theological terms, his soul. This he will do, for example, by recognizing as valid the intensities of his own experience, intensities of perception and appreciation of the world, intensities of insight and of exquisite expression. Such cognition will not help him escape the grave, but will, at least, make him aware of what he takes to it, of how sadly secret and unknown he will lie in the grave, suggesting by way of compensation at the melancholy hour that if he must leave all other men behind him, he was never fully and completely with them, and takes to the dust unique and private treasures more appropriately interred with and through him.

Here then are adumbrations of 'the ideal Jew', man among men, acquainted with the ways of living not only among, but with and in response to men, and not unaware of what he keeps from men and to himself, an individual in community, an identity at once at home and alien.

How does the ideal Jew live his life? He goes about his task, as one might expect, perplexed and questioning. He wonders what he ought to do and not to do, and asks himself to explain the commonplace and routine events, such as decency and thievery, kindness and callousness, regeneration and decay. In the day's events, he detects existential issues, hidden in them and sometimes best left hidden. If he has had a Jewish education, he finds words out of some sage's book that apply to these existential issues, that cast a different light upon them, or that may suggest, perhaps, insight into them, even an answer, however gnomic, to them. He is not, therefore, alone, the first and the last to ask, but is in conversation with others, listening at least to their words and responding to them through the uniqueness of his own question and his own experience, himself giving life to the dead, himself resurrecting the otherwise forgotten and worthless sentences out of the past. He draws, therefore, upon the accumulated 'wisdom' of the past, wisdom being a synonym for opinion sufficiently long ignored to be interesting to reconsider.

Jewish education is thus a profoundly humane inquiry, an effort to recreate community in age succeeding age, to preserve the private person within community, to guarantee the moral substance of the common life. It is a social task, and it is a cultural task, social in its direct application to the situation of Jews and men, cultural in its effort to enhance this situation through the establishment of existentially fruitful ways of conducting and contemplating life.

I shall describe, therefore, moments in which Jewish education is realized:

First, and most simply, if a man be not seen by any other and find a wallet in a railroad station phone booth: if, obeying more than mere moral impulse, he hears 'Don't steal,' or 'Return what your friend has lost,' or 'These are the finds that must be returned,' or see himself for an instant as a student of Salanter or a disciple of some long-dead figure known to him only through the lovely fables once spun and then retold, and if he make effort to find the owner, then he is a man and a Jew;

Second, if a man stand at the grave of his father, with David at his side in a valley of deep darkness, or with Solomon the aged king, at the end of a road from nowhere to nowhere, and if he respond to the unreasonable demand of his ancestors that then and there he pronounce a blessing and a hope for the speedy end of darkness and futility, then he is a man and a Jew;

Third, if a man contemplate the old age of others and their decaying bodies as occasion and vessel of golden and serene lessons about life, patiently honouring those who are no longer useful to him and forgiving those who did to him as he now does to his children, and if he find these rare capacities through obedience to the unnatural injunctions of his forebears to honour age and revere it, then he is a man and a Jew;

Fourth, if a man come to a moment of satisfaction and fulfilment and have the good taste to know how to be happy, if he find pleasure and preserve its integrity, neither misjudging its endurance nor misunderstanding its dimensions, and if he knows how and for what and when to express joy, and if he learn these things in the forms and gestures of his forebears, then he is a man and a Jew.

One need not multiply instances of existentially significant education, though one might do so through considering each element of Judaism, its literature and its festivals, its demands for action and demands for inaction, its imposition of rhythm upon the routines of life and its insistence on removing certain moments from those routines for the sake of inwardness, or contemplation, or cultivation of the soul or communication with being, or, in theological language, prayer. These instances will occur readily enough to anyone who is, in any sense at all and in any measure at all, a Jew. I only wish to suggest how Jewish education, as the task of creation of Jews out of the raw clay of unformed men by means of moulds of ancient design, is realized from time to time.

What are the consequences for Jewish education of the educational (more broadly, cultural) purposes that I have described? The first consequence, which is neither novel nor, alas, widely recognized, is that Jewish education is too important to be imparted to children, and yet, too significant to be withheld from them. They indeed ask the existential questions, because such questions are most obvious to those not yet protected from anxiety by routine. What to do? Teach the children what children can learn, and teach adults what adults can learn. Children can memorize, and they ought to be helped to exercise that extraordinary, but fleeting skill. They ought therefore to learn what can be learned by rote, such as language, including the language of liturgy and Scripture, so that these words will indeed recur when they are relevant to life. To learn language means, of course, to learn to use language for communication, for thought, and for creative purposes. They ought also to be initiated into memories, both personal and communal, so that they take up the bonds awaiting them, that eventually will tie them into community with unknown men long dead or not yet born. Thus the rites and rituals of Jewish life—the 'synagogue skills' to describe the matter technically—ought to be imparted to children. And when they wonder, they should be told that questions are in the world, and that the words and gestures they acquire contain within them deeper questions, or answers.

Jewish education, on the other hand, ought no longer to be regarded, if it ever was by any truly educated Jew, as a 'process' that comes to an end, or that ever reaches fulfilment or, even, fruition. The true description of the Jews ought to be 'learning men', and this must mean at the very least men who read books and talk about them, who even engage in formal study with teachers, knowing how to listen and learn, and even how to be silent and learn through contemplation. The 'ideal Jew' I described earlier is therefore a Jew who is not yet fully a Jew (and I do not mean this in merely a ritual sense), who sees life so differently from one day to the next that he must also seek knowledge or wisdom or understanding about it from one day to the next; who, moreover, seeks knowledge even when life does not demand it, or, indeed, especially so, because in the cultivation of his mind's skills, and in the increase of his own, however irrelevant treasure of knowledge and even information, he will find the means to cultivate his individuality, his capacity to perceive (in a personal way), his capacity to love (in a fraternal way), and his capacity to share community and to participate in the Jewish situation.

V

MOTIVATIONS FOR JEWISH LEARNING IN THE DIASPORA

I SHOULD LIKE to suggest answers to two questions: Why have people studied Hebrew and its associated disciplines, which for the sake of brevity I shall call 'Hebrew culture'; and, second, why ought they to study Hebrew. I am a historian and not a trained social scientist, and my descriptive effort is based only on the historian's power to observe and to describe what he thinks he sees.

In the past centuries, two distinct groups have interested themselves in Hebrew culture—Christians and Jews. Christian interest in Hebrew flowered in different periods, particularly during the patristic, early Renaissance, and Protestant eras. It was based on interest in Hebrew scriptures in the patristic and Protestant eras, and in Kabbalah during the Renaissance, in the belief that these writings contained the word of God, and in the expectation that closer understanding of Hebrew would yield a purer, more authentic Christianity. The Pauline thesis, that Christianity had superseded Judaism, stimulated keen interest in ancient scriptures. The results were a substantial achievement in scholarship, and widespread knowledge of scripture in the original tongue.

Present-day Christian interest is motivated, likewise, by interest in Hebrew scriptures. Hebrew literature and culture are generally wedged in between Mesopotamian and Egyptian studies in the Christian-Humanistic universities, and presented along with the classical literature of Greece and Rome as precursors of Christianity. This results in part from drawing conclusions from the vast silence on what happened in Israel after the first century C.E. In only a few universities is Hebrew studied as a living language, or the literature and history of Israel after Bar Kochba presented with competence. Indeed, where post-biblical Hebrew studies are pursued, one man alone is generally expected to offer whatever will be taught about the past twenty centuries. One man alone must have the complex disciplines needed to uncover the truth about the last 2,000 years, disciplines mastered in parallel fields of the same epoch by whole departments and faculties of philosophy, literature, history, and law.

Therefore, one may conclude that the interest of the humanistic West is still motivated by the religious archetypes of the preceding age, and that for the most part, even today, Hebrew is studied in so far as it is relevant to Christian *cultural*, if not specifically religious purposes.

We turn next to the question of past and present Jewish motivations to study Hebrew.

From the time that it ceased to be the living language of the Jewish people in the land of Israel, Hebrew was primarily a hieratic language. Viewed from its use for divine purposes, such as prayer, mastery of sacred texts, legal, homiletical, and exegetical pursuits, one may conclude that, with few, well-known exceptions, Hebrew literature before the Haskalah was not a profane literature, nor was Hebrew creativity divorced from Judaism. Hence Jewish interest in Hebrew culture had motivations similar to the Christian: Hebrew was the instrument of faith, and was cultivated almost entirely for sacred purposes. I do not ignore the influence of Hebrew language and literature upon the civilizations of Jews in various places, or on the development of their ethnic languages, whether Yiddish, Ladino, or Judeo-Persian. But since Jewish civilizations have been so centrally religious, it is difficult to explain the dominance of Hebrew, either in day-to-day affairs or in the curriculum of the schools, without reference to hieratic purposes.

Why do people study Hebrew today? Motivations have not greatly altered. Christian students study Hebrew because they want to read the Bible. Jews too learn Hebrew, when they do, mainly for hieratic purposes. It is studied for use in the synagogue, taught for use in the synagogue, and the kind of language that results is not substantially different from the Latin of the Roman Catholic churches. This is despite the valiant efforts of teachers and administrators of modern Hebrew schools, who have as their goal instruction in modern Hebrew for conversation and for reading modern literature. Even in the day-schools, or perhaps, especially there, the humanistic motive supplements religious concern, although this is usually more important to the teacher than to the student.

The lamentable tendency of the well-trained Hebrew school graduate to recite without understanding what he is reciting, and the even more regrettable assumption that mere recitation represents an act of sacred significance, are so widespread that one cannot dispute the essentially ritualistic character of Hebrew among those diaspora Jews who know it at all. Like the Tibetan Lhama who turns his prayer wheel, the Bar Mitzvah boy who chants his *haftarah* has performed an act of objective, independent, value virtually able to coerce God.

The exceptions to the rule that Hebrew culture is preserved mainly for its ritualistic (I cannot say here *religious*) value are those who study Hebrew because they want to go, or have been, to the State of Israel. In the university classroom, these students make great progress; those who actually study Hebrew in Israel achieve impressive results. But mainly, the efforts of past and future tourists and even immigrants produce insignificant results. Whether this motivation alone is sufficiently strong to yield significant mastery of the language, let alone capacity to use it creatively (that

58

is, to read for pleasure, to speak for communication, to write for greater power) is open to doubt.

To summarize: Hebrew has been studied as a means of mastering the religious segment of its literature for ultimately passive, that is, non-creative purposes: in order, among Christians, to read the Hebrew scriptures and scrolls; and additionally, among Jews, to read the Siddur, the specified *haftarot* and the Torah. We cannot regret these motivations, or ignore their cultural implications. It is entirely possible that mere ability to read the Siddur and *haftarah* is all that can be hoped for from the vast majority of diaspora Jews, and that reaching this relatively humble goal will represent a major cultural achievement by the diaspora Jewish community.

In addition to the study of Hebrew for religious purposes, I hope we shall see new awareness of the importance of studying Hebrew for other, complementary reasons.

There are additional motivations, other goals, that are just as important and useful as those relating to the liturgy, even though we all recognize that these motivations may touch the lives of relatively few individuals or communities.

First, the powerful motivation that Hebrew is the language of the Creator is not likely to move those who have other theologies, or no theology at all. Today many loyal Jews do not expect, when they reach Heaven, to be greeted with the word 'shalom'. In fact, they do not expect to go to heaven, or anywhere else. We need to articulate a this-worldly motivation for the diaspora Jew to learn Hebrew.

For many, particularly those who are in colleges, universities, and part of a cultural group, Hebrew can be an important mode of individuation, of achievement and discovery of personal identity among the undifferentiated mass of Americans. As our theologians, such as Will Herberg, and sociologists, such as Nathan Glazer and Marshall Sklare, have already taught us, one of the existentially significant needs of Western men living in cosmopolitan centres is to find a way of answering the question, 'What

59

are you?' Jonah's answer, 'I am a Hebrew' remains peculiarly appropriate. Dispassionate study of Hebrew and its
literature may yield a viable and appropriate answer for
the alienated intellectual. Herberg tells us that the Jew will
answer, 'I am Jewish', whether he has a theology or not.

Study of Hebrew literature, particularly in the modern
period, will provide antecedents, grandparents, for one who
is Jewish without Judaism; it will show him that he is part
of a rich and creative tradition of Jews who broke with
religion, and remained Jews. He will find that others have
asked the questions that perplex him, and have experi-
mented, with greater or lesser degrees of success, with
answers to these questions. Modern Hebrew literature, and
modern Hebrew thought particularly, but not only on
Zionist and other sociological issues, will provide for the
secularist-intellectual a source of values, of self-awareness
and self-identification no less fruitful than earlier Hebrew
literature provides for those whose orientation remains
religious.

If the concept of Torah relates to all of Jewish cultural
achievement in every age, then the scripture in Deuteronomy applies no less to the secular Hebraist in the
diaspora than to the religious Hebraist: 'Keep them and do
them, for that will be your wisdom and your understanding
in the sight of the peoples, who, when they hear all these
statutes will say, Surely this great nation is a wise and
understanding people' (Deut. 4:6–7).

There is nothing so pathetic as the Jew without roots,
and yet where will the secularist, atheist Jew find roots
outside the fields cultivated for two centuries by his spiritual
forefathers? Jewish university youth, in particular, will find
in modern literature a way to think about their perplexities.
In their studies of modern Western civilization they acquire
an attitude of genteel anti-Semitism. They read Pound and
Eliot and even Toynbee, and come to admire the achievements of a world they did not make; yet they are Jews,
and they choose not to ignore or escape this fact.

Told that the Jews also contributed to the civilization of the West, they perceive that these contributions are tangential either to the West or to Judaism; if Freud, Marx, and Einstein were Jews, they were certainly not like the Jews our university students know about, and their achievements were not specifically and directly the products of Judaism. They tend to think 'We Jews are the greatest' or 'We Jews are nothing', and neither viewpoint is likely to yield truth. Where will they find their brothers and their fathers, if not among the creators of the *Haskalah* and of modern Hebrew literature? And how will they discover them, if not in their own language and idiom?

Second, the continued existence of the Jewish community in the diaspora requires intensive cultivation of Hebrew letters, for a thoroughly practical reason. That community rests upon the loyalties and sentiments of two older generations of Jews whose experience is not duplicated, for good or ill, among the third and fourth generations. Western Jewry prides itself upon its institutional, philanthropic achievements. These achievements were based upon the loyalties and commitments of European, mainly East European, Jews who were educated under very different circumstances.

To them being Jewish bore numerous and complex implications about themselves, about their relationship to the world, about their understanding of life; those circumstances, and concomitant implications, are simply not available to diaspora Jews today. My generation, the third, does not remember the *shtetl*, even though we read *Life Is With People*. We do not remember *bubbee's kneidlach*, or Yiddish; or Jewish homelessness and frustration. My father's generation lived through the trauma of the European tragedy and Zion redeemed. They felt that they participated in a great historical and spiritual adventure, because they were Jews. Many of his generation felt that they had endured the *havlei mashiah*, the pangs of redemption, and now witnessed the beginnings of redemption itself in the rise of the State

61

of Israel. The Jewish community has lived for fifty years on the capital of Eastern Europe, in the first place, and of historical disaster and triumph, in the second. But the old capital, based upon powerful collective historical and social experience, is used up. The young diaspora Jew needs to generate new 'capital'. Where can he look?

The powerful experiences of Jewish learning and intellectualism are still unexplored by much of Western Jewry. The tremendous thirst for learning that remains characteristic of large numbers of Jews, can lead once again to the study of the Torah understood in its broadest sense: the study of Hebrew language, literature, and civilization. The earlier generations of Western Jews were 'birthright' Jews, because the mere fact that they were Jews provided an identity, and a purpose for being, in a world where that fact was significant. The newer generations may become Jews by choice, by cultural, educational, and religious acts, because participation in the Jewish and Hebrew cultural adventure will provide for them an identity and a purpose for being in a world that increasingly measures the *man*, not his ancestry.

I affirm the beneficent influence of other civilizations upon Jewish civilization, and find it difficult to recognize a setting in which Jews were able to isolate themselves from other groups and cultures *and* at the same time to maintain their own capacity to prosper, to create within their own setting. On the contrary, I find that the Jewish historical ages of most impressive, abiding cultural achievement have been precisely those in which Jews were most deeply involved in and responsive to the heritage of alien civilizations, whether this involvement was affirmative, as in the Hellenistic world, medieval Spain, and Western Europe, in the 19th century, or negative, as in the Mosaic and prophetic periods, and to some degree, East-European Judaism as well.

Hence my ideal for diaspora Jewry is clear-cut and precise. I look forward to a Jewish community in the West that responds to the civilization of the modern West, and to its peculiar legacy from earlier civilizations, both Jewish and otherwise; a community whose creativity uses both the artifacts of Western experience and the raw material of Jewish existence, a community that is truly capable of responding to cultural and social challenges of the contemporary setting in a historically authentic manner. There is nothing quite so beautiful as the fragile blossom of the *golah*, nourished in alien soil and bringing forth the flower of ancient seed.

I know nothing so unique, so splendid in human achievement as that much lamented and tragic community of German Judaism, so deeply German and so identifiably and creatively Jewish; that community which provided most ideas that motivate American Jewish religion today, whether Reform, from Geiger; Conservative, from Frankel and Graetz; or Orthodox, from Hirsch. I want to see in the West the development of humanistic, cultured diaspora Jews, whose Judaism is informed by the Judaism of other lands and ages, shaped by the classical moulds, nourished by the resources of this enduring people; and whose nationalism is in far more than a political sense the product of Western, particularly British and American, history and literature. Judaism will emerge from the Western experience profoundly transformed. Jewish civilization can never be the same, just as Judaism could never be the same after the achievements of 19th-century German Jewry.

It must be self-evident that if the national loyalty of the Western Jew is founded upon more than mere acquaintance with the history of his native country, study and appreciation of its literature, participation in the cultural, economic, social and political life—even at the frontiers of that life, the Judaism of the modern, Western Jew is not well established at all. For the most part, the British and American Jew is 'Jewish' only by contrast to the Gentile. He is a social fact, a sociological entity. But whether he is a Jew or not, either in the mass or among the creative minority, is open to question. In numerous, barely articulated ways, he is obviously Jewish. But when we discuss the 'Jewishness' of the diaspora Jew, we must still look for inexact and highly sentimental definitions of that Jewishness. We say he is Jewish because of his devotion to certain aspects of liberal idealism, or philanthropy. But these bases of definition do not permit close examination or evaluation by precise criteria, such as direct reference by the Jew himself to the literature and resources of his people. He is in this sense a passive Jew, not a creative one, for his 'Jewishness' or Judaism is the result not of conscious, culturally aware action, but rather the consequence of historical realities to which he responds passively and unselfconsciously.

The issue before us, therefore, is one faced by rabbis, teachers, social and communal workers, novelists, scholars and sociologists, day by day and week by week: how shall we become Jews not passively but actively, existentially, and creatively?

There is one way only, and that is by acquiring for our own purposes the historical literature of the Jewish people, through translation if necessary, but more usefully, more authentically, through mastery of its language and idiom. And that literature was, and is, and always will be in the Hebrew language. Jews have created in many languages, but they have preserved their creations only in Hebrew. Hebrew is not only international, as the instrument of Jewish unity today, but it is also the language of the abiding, enduring achievements of the Jewish past, upon which we base our Jewish civilization today, and from which we hope to derive the raw material of Jewish creativity for the future.

Hebrew is—in the most prosaic possible sense—the language of eternity: if Ezekiel had written in Babylonian, Ezra in Avestan, Mar Samuel in Pahlavi, and Maimonides and Saadye in Arabic only; if the literature of Hassidism and Kabbalah had not found appropriate vocabulary in Hebrew, who then would read these books? Who would

64

draw insight from their authors' insight? For whom would their words continue to live, to illumine new and unexpected perplexities?

Hence, to answer the original question, the proper motivation for the pursuit of Hebrew letters in the diaspora is eminently practical. It is, first of all, to assure that we shall have access, as individuals and particularly as thoughtful, creative men and women, to the ideas, idiom and insight of those who lived as Jews before us in other lands and ages. It is, second, to assure that we shall shape ourselves and our communities into authentic representations of the Jewish cultural and historical experience, by responding to these books and words on the basis of understanding and direct experience, and by gaining guidance from them. It is, finally, to be certain that we shall add to this body of historical human experience, and the literature that records it, so that elsewhere today and in time to come, our particular achievements may find recognition, our insights may find understanding, our failures may find sympathy. Hebrew letters represent too broad a humanistic concern to be limited by the severely narrow definitions enclosing religion today, or to be restricted to the cultic and ritualistic confessional reservation. Our motive must find definition in the broader interests that impel all humanistic enterprise. I ought to add, finally, a statement on the significance of Jewish education for the study and transmission of Western civilization, of which the Jews have been an integral part for so long.

Because of improved communications, men of the West are confronted with whole new cultures, the cultures of the Eastern peoples such as the Arabs, Iranians, the Indians, the South Asians, the Chinese, and the Japanese. We meet entirely different ways of living life and understanding the world. One major result has been that the common understanding of what Western Civilization is and means has changed. We have not only begun to broaden our concept of ways to live life and to understand the world, but we have, in fact, begun to compare and to contrast those of our own world with those of the rest of humanity. One genuinely useful way of extending our intellectual horizons is surely to consider the intellectual heritage of the Jewish people, that have lived in the West for two thousand years, that have in some measure shared the values and ideas of the West, and that have yet preserved another, quite different way of seeing the world. The Jews have, throughout the history of the Golah, learned to live with contrasting and, sometimes, even with conflicting cultures; they have lived in two civilizations, and in one world. Their intellectual life has paralleled, has shared, and has, also, diverged from, the intellect and imagination of the West at different periods and in different aspects. For this reason, if for no other, Jewish social and intellectual experience from the beginnings of recorded history to the present day is important, interesting, and relevant to Western civilization.

If the Jewish people had met utter destruction at the hands of the German Nazis between 1933 and 1945, the humane West would doubtless take deep interest in the history and literature and philosophy of these ancient, tragic men. What could be more pathetic or more tragic, or, therefore, more interesting to men of culture than the story of what happened between Abraham and Auschwitz? Indeed there are some places where it is more respectable to exhume the dead than to examine the living. But the Jewish people live, endure, create. They have produced records of a continuing social experience, of a fundamental idea, of a complex culture; they have preserved and enhanced a language, a literature; and, in a paradoxical way, they have endured a triumphant history. Serious study of the civilization of the Jewish people must, therefore, be of value.

If therefore, the Jews have had some insight into the life of the mind, into the conduct and explanation of human existence, into the means to create culture and to build civilization, then that vision ought to be shared in the

66

places where the lights still burn and where men's eyes are still open. This is an age of descending darkness, yet the dark is not so black that it cannot be illumined by the slender, flickering flame that glows from the books dictators must burn, and from the lives of the living people, so frail and alone, before whom tyrants must tremble.

VI

SCHOLARS AND MACHINES

HUMANE SCHOLARS ARE the most unmechanized of men. Long ago they shut the study door to the industrial revolution. Sitting inside with stubby pencil and scratch-sheet, they depend on an antique technology. However, the electronic computer now apparently threatens scholars with technological unemployment. With the computer one scholar in a few hours does the work of whole universities of scholars in many years. The computer classifies and compares, organizes and arranges. It prepares a concordance of a literature or a whole language in a matter of hours. In the past more than one academic reputation was built on a lifetime of patient, semi-technical drudgery of this sort. The computers can even propose emendations to difficult texts and carry out effectively work done today by armies of scholars. They can almost think.

The IBM 704 electronic computer, for example, prepared a concordance for the Dead Sea Scrolls, transposing the prose into a series of mathematical relationships. The machine was used to analyze the many *lacunae* in the Scrolls, referring to the words preceding and following a difficult text, and scanning thousands of other words to find those that most nearly fit the context. The accuracy of the machine was tested by blocking out portions of familiar text. It was found that the computer could accurately recover as many as five consecutive words.

This method, first used to compile a concordance to the

works of St. Thomas Aquinas, was developed in 1949 by
Father Roberto Busa, of the Jesuit College of the Aloisianum
in Gallarate, Italy, and an IBM engineer, Paul Tasman.
The work on the Scroll concordance, also directed by
Father Busa, began at Gallarate where technicians reduced
nearly thirty thousand words to IBM cards. A card was
punched for each word, giving its location, by line, scroll,
column, and sequence, and any distinguishing characteristics. In two hours the cards were converted to two reels of
magnetic tape by the IBM 704 computer in New York, and
the final alphabetical summary was printed by the machine
in Hebrew at about 150 lines a minute.

The IBM 704 computer is now working on abstracts of
scientific and technical articles. The articles are read into
the machine, which analyzes them sentence by sentence
and selects the significant material for reproduction on an
electronic printer. The process, called *Auto Abstracting*,
follows preset instructions, for (as the IBM people admit)
the computer is at present incapable of intellectual compre-
hension. It can only treat words as physical entities, determining significance by measuring the frequency with which
they appear both individually and in various combinations.

The scholars, having come late into the machine age,
may well learn from the experience of others. When the
camera was invented in the nineteenth century, artists faced
technological obsolescence, for it seemed that everything
they had achieved with oils and canvas, the camera could
do better on film. Portraits, landscapes, indeed the precise
representation of reality in every aspect, might be better
executed by a mediocre photographer than by the most
skilful artist. What was left for the artist but to abandon
his oils for photography?

Some indeed did this and demonstrated that the camera
too was worthy of great artistry. Others re-examined the
proper task for their art and, facing the challenge of photography, abandoned the technical representation of reality for
the representation of what man actually sees and the artist

truly reproduces. They discovered that art never actually represented reality at all, for the eye sees much more than the canvas contains. They recognized that even the most photographic of artists actually selects and represents a very tentative segment of reality. Exhilarated by this new vision, they explored the infinitely subtle world of colour and light; they met for the first time the challenge of formal symbolism; they surrendered to the camera its own, the commonplace view of things, and claimed for themselves what in truth had always been theirs, the impression of their vision and the expression of their souls. Art became in time the expression of self-conscious human vision.

What then is the meaning of the electronic computer for humane letters?

It means, first of all, that some humanists, particularly in philology and text-criticism, will have to master the techniques which make the machine a useful tool for their study. They will have to think through the kinds of work the machine can do best and indeed to discover new uses for it. As the technicians become experienced in preparing concordances and in proposing to the machine certain essentially mathematical problems in text criticism, they may well discover new capabilities for the computer. They will certainly find the machine useful in preparing critical texts of ancient manuscripts.

The technicians will on the other hand also need to determine the computer's limitations. Is technical mastery of the computer even sufficient to prepare a proper concordance? The story of the Biblical concordance raises doubt that machines can provide much more than technical accuracy and mechanical efficiency.

The first concordance, prepared by Rabbi Nathan b. Kalonymus of Arles in Provence in 1437–1445, ought to have sufficed, for it listed all the Biblical uses of the several thousand words in the Hebrew scriptures. It did indeed provide a basic pattern followed by future workers (and, by the way, was the first Jewish work to accept the division of the Bible into chapter and verse begun by the Vulgate). It was republished seven times in the two centuries after the discovery of printing and for the first time in 1523, only three decades after the invention of movable type.

The work of preparing a concordance to the Bible, however, was by no means complete. R. Isaac Nathan's work was revised by Johann Buxtorf the Elder of Basel who added different derivative roots, nominal and verbal forms, and rearranged words according to a grammatical scheme. His son added the Aramaic portions. This work itself was revised in the nineteenth century by Julius Furst who published in 1840 a complete revision of Buxtorf's work. He rearranged the words according to his own theory of the origin and form of words; Furst held the theory of his pupil, Franz Delitzsch, that Semitic languages are closely connected with Indo-Germanic roots. This theory led deviously to listing the word *Dam* (blood) under the category *Adam* (man). Needless to say, Furst's concordance posed certain difficulties to later scholars. It had the virtue of providing an etymological index, a list of proper names, a list of Phoenicio-Punic proper names, and so on. It was not however exactly the last word on etymology.

When Solomon Mandelkern began to prepare *his* concordances to the Bible, he began by presenting trenchant and compelling criticism of earlier work. He added variants from the Aramaic and Greek translations; he concerned himself with unclear texts, suggesting possible meanings for difficult passages. He rearranged the order in which words were listed. He completed the references which Furst and his predecessors had given only in part. He corrected errors in determining the roots of Hebrew verbs and nouns. He added those words which are used only once in Scripture. Somehow no one earlier thought they mattered. He corrected Furst's grammar. In short he prepared what amounted to a wholly new piece of work.

Mandelkern spent the rest of his life improving his concordance. In 1909 Prof. Sveyn Hermer published a *Ver-*

besserung, an improvement, for Mandelkern's concordance. A second edition was published in 1925, incorporating corrections and improvements proposed by many scholars.

The latest concordance to the Bible, a revised and improved edition of Mandelkern, was published just four years ago. Five centuries have passed, and scholars still do not have a complete, final concordance to the few thousand words of the Bible.

How could the electronic computer have hastened this work? It could have provided greater accuracy (Mandelkern complains of thousands of errors in classification found in earlier concordances). It could perhaps have hastened the actual labour of arranging references. It could have done nothing else, for, as the story of the Biblical concordance indicates, the work depends on the scholars. The scholars have to determine the principles of grammar, of syntax; they have to uncover the mysteries of incomprehensible texts and decide on variant readings. The machine is able to grasp the principles of organization and comparison they devise and to generalize these principles throughout a vast body of material. But it also reproduces their errors with dreadful accuracy.

The sensational news about the computer and the Scrolls becomes therefore rather less decisive for humane scholarship. It will certainly no longer suffice for a scholar to make his name through extraordinary persistence. He will no longer have a strong claim to the mind of learning man by competence in comparing variant readings and producing mechanical 'text criticism'. Remarkable feats of memory are obsolete. The machine remembers better and longer. It holds together facts; used properly, it can create bibliographies and reproduce whatever it is told.

Scholarship is in this way obsolete, if by scholarship one understands formidable efficiency in collecting and classifying everything that is remotely relevant to anything. The question the machine raises is not, however, what will be the new role for humane letters, for the concordance-story indicates the limitations of the computer. The machine does on the other hand reaffirm the claim of the humanities to tasks which have always been their own: the search for wisdom.

If scholarship means the pursuit of wisdom in a rigorous and rational manner, then scholarship will never become obsolete until clear thinking is out of fashion and men find no more serious questions to ask.

In truth the scholars who need now to watch out that they are not put out of work by machines were never scholars at all, but careerists, the handservants of scholars. They are those who made a profession and a technique out of the obligation of everyone to seek a wise and understanding heart. The genuine scholar finds on the contrary that the new machines bring him a new freedom from drudgery and pedantry, freedom to think and to explore. The scholar is now freer to undertake the responsibilities that were always his. He is now to some extent unburdened of the task of providing the trivial kind of information to be gotten from technical apparatus; within wide limits the machines will, more and more, get this for him. He can recover the sense of purpose in his study that humane learning promises every man, to recover and ponder the memories and wise insights of the mind of man.

Humane letters were once a search for human values. So they can be once again. Humanists were once not professionals, almost exclusively concerned with technical knowledge. Once upon a time, this would have seemed a contradiction to the whole purpose of the study of man. The humane scholar concerned himself with man, his wisdom, heritage, and worth. His study was not professional but the obligation of serious amateurs. Humane letters were once an exciting experience. They spoke to the questions of men busy with living. When for example the founders of 'Jewish Science' pored over texts, they were intoxicated with the idea that their discoveries were immediately relevant to contemporary Judaism. (On this account admittedly

73

they produced some remarkably myopic theories). Human-ists once again will find they need to speak on the issues confronting living men. They will draw freely from the wisdom of the past but also form their own insights into the past and into their own times. They need no longer fear that to speak relevantly means to cease to be an authentic scholar.

As humane letters become once again the domain of all who seek after wisdom, technical scholarship in its narrow and contemporary sense will be considered a means toward an intellectual end but not a sufficient purpose. As humane scholars turn their attention once again to human issues, they may well learn from traditional Jewish students of the Talmud. Rigorous and precise, these sages may have come upon esoteric information, but they were never trivial, they never lost their sense of relevance to the perplexities of men. Though they did not seek to solve questions that were immediately pressing and practical, they were always aware that the ultimate issue of their study was life and its meaning and conduct. They pondered in a thousand arguments the tension between revealed truth, as they held it, and human affairs. They concerned themselves with remote issues, but they discovered in them truth for the immediate situation. Beyond and above all else, their study was an act of morality. The rabbis and sages poured their lives into the study of the *Talmud*. They consecrated themselves and made their souls holy to the cause of the mind.

Yet the rabbis too were men and felt the call to do, to gain power and use it. They resisted mundaneness because their studies were worth their whole being. It was worth their while to do nothing but study *Talmud*, because the study of *Talmud* was for them life itself. Thinking was creating. It was doing and making and the achievement of the intellect and—they would say, uniquely—the final worthiness of man.

Machines will, one hopes, bring about such a new vision of the tasks of humane scholarship: to seek wisdom. They will help man to recover his sense for the austerity and rigour of his intellect. By freeing him from petty tasks that weary his mind, they will probably make triviality obsolete; they will certainly show that the doctoral dissertation commonly demanded represents at best skilled craftsmanship but surely not art.

The machines will certainly not make genius obsolete nor put thinkers out of work. They will help us to see, however, that thinking is not to be reserved for technicians and professionals. The quality of insight of humane scholarship will be reconsidered, for with the abandoning of technicism and professionalism, humanities lose the claim to positive, compelling truth. Humane letters surely regain, however, an ancient and mature vision, that scholarship is the search into the very substance of life. Then the humane search for truth becomes, in itself and in its consequences, a statement of being. Then indeed scholars will come to see the truth of the ancient dictum, 'If thou hast wrought much in the study of Torah take no credit to thyself, for to this end wast thou created.'

VII

LEARNING AND DEEDS

A Life of Rabbi Tarfon

RABBI TARFON, WHO lived ca. 50–130 C.E., was one of the
Jewish religious teachers called *Tannaim* who gathered at the
coastal town of Yavneh (Jamnia) during the years between
the destruction of the Second Temple (in 70 C.E.) and the
disastrous rebellion of Bar Kokhba (132 C.E.). While he has
occasionally been identified with the Trypho of Justin
Martyr's dialogue in Ephesus at about 150 C.E., there is
little evidence to support such an identification.[1] Tarfon's
importance was, rather, as a member of the Yavneh academy,
and as teacher or colleague of such men of primary and
abiding significance as Akiba, Eliezer ben Hyrcanus, Joshua
ben Hananiah, and Judah bar Ilai.

Rabbi Tarfon was direct and straightforward, not much
given to fantasy and impatient with subtle theorizing. With
unambiguous wisdom, he would seize the crucial issue and
decide it. He would teach 'The day is short, the task is great,
the workmen sluggish, the reward ample, the master
insistent. Thine it may not be to complete the task, neither
art thou free to desist from it.'[2] He was not a master of
legend-spinning, and was ill at ease when discussion called
for free play of imagination. When the rabbis mused 'Who
is rich?', some might come to high moral sentiment, but not
Rabbi Tarfon. 'Who is rich? One who is satisfied with his
lot'. Rabbi Akiba says, 'One who has a willing wife.' Rabbi

Tarfon says, 'One who has a hundred vineyards and a hundred fields and a hundred slaves to work them[3]'. His colleagues recognized this weakness, and they did not look to him for flights of fancy. He was not adept at seeking hidden meaning in the words of scripture.[4] He could indeed pun with the best of a generation that joked through puns,[5] but he would rebuke a colleague for talking 'nonsense.' When the noted Agadist, Eliezer of Modin, sat before Rabbi Tarfon and the elders, he expounded; 'The manna which came down to Israel was sixty cubits high!'

'O Modite, how long will you rake together words to bring up against us?' Rabbi Tarfon exclaimed.

'But master, I am only expounding scriptural verse.[6]'

When Rabbi Tarfon himself tried his hand at Agada, he proved inept. Once it was asked: 'Who is it who "does righteousness at *all* times" (Psalm 106:3)?'

'Can it be those who teach children Bible and Mishnah?' Rabbi Tarfon answered.

'But do they not eat and drink and sleep? They surely do not do righteousness at *all* times?'

'Can it,' he countered, 'be those who write out tefillin and mezuzot?'

'But,' they objected, 'do they too not eat and drink and sleep? Who is it then that does righteousness at all times?'

'You must say that it is he who brings up an orphan in his house, for the orphan is always provided with the clothes that he gave him and hence, the righteousness is, in effect, always being done.'

'But,' they answered, 'would you say that he does not sleep naked at night? [It was customary to sleep naked.] We still need the Modite[7]!'

He was therefore a man of plain commonsense; he was not simple, but he probed with simple directness into a complex problem. How did he reason out a moral riddle? A rumour went out that certain Galileans had killed a man. The suspects came to Rabbi Tarfon and said: 'Will the master hide us?'

'How should I act? Should I not hide you, those who avenge the blood will see you (and execute vengeance whether you are properly tried or not). Should I hide you, I should be acting contrary to the teaching of the rabbis; As to slander, though one should not believe it, one should take note of it. (Further, if the report is true, I have no right to shield you). 'Go', he concluded, 'and hide yourselves!⁸'

In complex legal issues he would reason from an obvious premise to a clear conclusion. He dealt in such a manner with the following parallel cases: if a man betrothes one of five women and does not know which he has betrothed and each states that she is the betrothed, he must give a letter of divorce to each of them, and, leaving the marriage-money among them; he withdraws, according to Rabbi Tarfon. Rabbi Akiba objects: This is not a way to lead a man out of the toils of sin; rather, he must give to each of them both a letter of divorce and the marriage-money. Again, if a man robbed one of five persons without knowing which he had robbed and he wishes to return the theft, he may set down the stolen article among the claimants and depart, according to Rabbi Tarfon. Rabbi Akiba objects: This is not a way to lead a man out of the toils of sin; rather he must restore the appropriate article to each claimant.⁹

In each case Rabbi Tarfon follows the path of clear reason: the thief stole one object, he need return but one; the distraught suitor betrothed but one woman, he need pay marriage-money to but one. Let the claimants negotiate their claim; this is, after all, not unreasonable, since the thief did *not* steal from four of the claimants, the suitor did not betrothe four of the women, and at least some claimants are in the toils of sin for claiming that he did. Rabbi Akiba reasons more subtly, and more justly: a thief has committed a crime and wants to make recompense. If he returns one object to five claimants, it is likely to be divided among them, since there is no way of substantiating any one claim. Hence the one true claimant would only receive a fifth of his property, and the final result of the theft is not altered. If each claimant receives the full amount of the theft, the true claimant at least will not suffer; but otherwise the honest man still loses to dishonesty. The same reasoning applies to the case of the five affianced: the fiance did, after all, betrothe someone; if he was so careless as not to notice which woman he betrothed, he ought to be penalized five times in order that the real victim suffers no loss.

In abstract and complex issues of legal theory, Rabbi Tarfon had a tendency to avoid unnecessary 'theorizing'. For instance, if a man vows to become a Nazir (to take upon himself for a given period certain vows of abstinence), Rabbi Tarfon held that he must do so unconditionally and unequivocally. This avoids scholastic inquiry into situations such as this: if six people were walking along the road, and saw someone coming toward them, and one said: I declare myself a Nazir if it is not so-and-so, and another said: if it is so-and-so, and a third: I declare myself a Nazir if one of you is a Nazir, and a fourth: I declare myself a Nazir if neither of you is a Nazir, and a fifth, if both of you are Nazirs, and a sixth, if all of you are Nazirs – if this happened, Bet Shamai declares: all six are Nazirites; Bet Hillel rules: Only those whose words are confirmed become Nazirites; and Rabbi Tarfon rules: not one of them becomes a Nazir.[10] Tortuous cases such as this are excluded under the simple principle that all vows of this sort must be unconditional and unequivocal.

Rabbi Tarfon would likewise accept humanity as an argument in law, while his colleagues insisted that 'logic must pierce the mountain.' If a man died, Rabbi Tarfon taught, leaving a wife, a creditor, and heirs, and he left a deposit or loan in possession of others, this deposit should be given to the weakest of them. Rabbi Akiba countered: No pity must be shown in a matter of law, but the deposit is given to the heir whose claim is the strongest.[11]

Not only is humanity an argument in law, but Rabbi Tarfon was also willing for the law to recognize the result of an extra-legal device. According to strict law, a *mamzer*

79

might never affect the legalization of his seed. Rabbi Tarfon taught that a *mamzer* might purify his descendants from this taint, so that they might marry legitimately. How? If a *mamzer*-freeman marries a bondmaid (which is, in the first place, not legal), her children will be his slaves, and he may free them. The children of a bondmaid need not show paternity. Hence the children would be both free and legitimate. Rabbi Tarfon suggested that the most felicitous means to carry out the marriage would be for the *mamzer* to marry in a place where he is unknown; the deed, once done, is done and the law will recognize his offspring as legitimate.[12] Rabbi Tarfon accepted the strict demands of logic, on the other hand, when logic would assert the humane, just as he denied logic when a human being would suffer.[13]

'A man is duty-bound to attend upon four scholars, such as Rabbi Eliezer, Rabbi Joshua, Rabbi Tarfon, and Rabbi Akiba.[14]' The disciple who came to Rabbi Tarfon was fortunate indeed. He was honest and did not conceal impatience; but in his gruff affection for students and colleagues, he dealt openly and honestly with all about him. If a student made a sound comment, he would exclaim, 'A knop and a flower' (quoting Exodus 25:33, 'It is well ordered like a knop and its flower') but if a student spoke nonsense, he would exclaim, 'My son shall not go down with you' (Genesis 42:38, punning on b'ni", my son, and "binah," understanding, that is to say, "I don't go along with you[15]"). He could be highly impatient: when his sister's sons sat in ignorant silence before him, he quoted the verse, 'And Abraham took another wife, and her name was Johanni' (Genesis 25:1).

The boys exclaimed, 'But it is written "Keturah".'

'That's just what you are, children of Keturah,' he answered; that is to say, you who cannot discuss law intelligently may be children of Abraham, but not of Sarah but of Keturah, an inferior breed![16]

His impatience was matched by impulsive generosity. Once he said to Rabbi Akiba: 'Go and buy for us a field that we may labour in the Torah and support ourselves from that field,' and he gave him six hundred silver coins. Since Rabbi Tarfon himself held large estates, he probably wanted Rabbi Akiba to live from the investment himself. Rabbi Akiba however took the money and gave it to the students and teachers who labour in the study of Torah. After some time Rabbi Tarfon asked Rabbi Akiba: 'Have you bought that field I told you to get?'

'Yes,' he replied.

'Can you show it to me?'

'Yes,' and he took him, and showed him schools of children and teachers labouring in the study of Torah. Rabbi Tarfon asked: 'But does a man give away anything for nothing? Where is the money's equivalent?'

Rabbi Akiba answered: 'It is with David, king of Israel, of whom it is written, "He has scattered abroad, he hath given to the needy, his righteousness (charity) endures for ever" (Psalms 112:9).[17]'

He had the humility to admit to his students that he did not know the answer to a question. Once the students asked him whether it is permitted to move the carcass of a beast that died during the festival, and whether *hallah* which became defiled (and which may not even be used as fuel during the festival) may be moved, and he went into the Academy and inquired and found that neither object may be moved. A century later it was pointed out that the sages who had answered Rabbi Tarfon themselves had erred.[18] His dealings with his family also were characterized by humility and kindness, and he was gallant to the weaker sex. Once, it is told, when he sat teaching his students a bride passed by. He told the students to bring her into his house and to have his mother and wife anoint and wash the bride, and to arrange the customary dances before her to make her rejoice until she was to go to her husband's house.[19] (That is not to say that he was a feminist; on the contrary, he taught that a termagant may be divorced without paying the marriage-money to her. And who is a termagant? A woman whose voice can be heard

by her neighbours when she speaks inside her own house.[20])
In days of famine he betrothed three hundred women (some
think it was only three) so that they could eat the priestly
tithes reserved for priests and their families.[21] Fables were
told of his humility toward his mother. It is said that Rabbi
Tarfon, a man who held many servants, would bend down to
let his mother ascend to her bed by stepping on his back.
When she took a walk in the courtyard on Sabbath, he
would place his hands under her feet to protect her until she
reached her couch. Once when he was sick, the scholars came
to visit him, and his mother said to them: 'Pray for my son
Tarfon, for he is wont to honour me, even too much!'

'And what does he do for you?'

She told them the story of his kindness on the Sabbath.
They answered: 'Even if he had done so a thousand thousand
times, still the honour for parents of which the Torah spoke
would not yet be fulfilled!'[22]

He was a loving father to his wife and children. It is
written: 'A man ought to make his wife and children merry
on the festival of Passover. And with what ought he to make
them merry? With wine.' To this Rabbi Judah bar Ilai,
Rabbi Tarfon's faithful student, objected: 'A man ought to
make women happy with what is fitting for them, for
example, roasted ears of corn and doves, and children with
what is fitting for them, for example, nuts and almonds. For
this is just what Rabbi Tarfon used to do.'[23]

This then was his way of dealing with abstract problems
and with everyday associates: direct and commonsensical
with the one, gruff and kind with the other.

The saddest men in history are those whose names are
joined in the mind of the future with those of men greater
than themselves. Rabbi Tarfon is known to the ages as Rabbi
Akiba's sometime teacher and colleague. The personalities
of the two men differed very profoundly. Rabbi Akiba was
subtle and complex, both in matters of law and in human
relationships. For example, both men would, as leading
figures in the academy, visit the sick and dying in their

midst. In these visits, the contrast between the two men becomes clear: Rabbi Tarfon brought sweet, simple, and direct good wishes, while Rabbi Akiba delivered a complex and stern message of strength.

When Rabbi Eliezer ben Hyrcanus fell ill, Rabbi Tarfon told him: 'You are more precious to Israel than the rain, for rain is precious in this world while you are precious for us in this world and in the world to come.' [As a result of Rabbi Eliezer's teaching, Israel would enjoy this world and the next.] Rabbi Akiba continued: 'Suffering is precious, because it makes atonement for the sufferer.' The sick man answered: 'Help me up so that I may hear the words of my disciple Akiba, who has said "Suffering is precious".'[24]

Rabbi Tarfon did not possess Rabbi Akiba's acumen and intellect. He would err, he would hear and forget what he heard; he would see an event and forget the details from which law could be determined. Not so Rabbi Akiba; his logical and powerful mind never failed him; he would make straight the crooked and clarify the unclear. Indeed few men could have provided more than a foil to such genius. Very often Rabbi Tarfon would say, 'May I bury my children if this is not a perverted teaching, which the hearer heard wrongly . . .' and Rabbi Akiba would answer, 'I shall amend this teaching so that the words of the sages remain valid;'[25] or he would exclaim, 'May I bury my children if I have not heard a distinction in this matter, yet I cannot explain what it is,' and Rabbi Akiba would answer without boast, 'I shall explain the distinction,' and he did so many times. Rabbi Tarfon would acknowledge: 'By the service of the Temple, you have not deviated right or left. I heard and yet could not explain, while you reason the matter out and agree with my hearsay. O Akiba, who parts from you parts from life itself!'[26] Rabbi Tarfon did not simply tender a graceful compliment when he said to Rabbi Akiba: 'Of thee, Akiba, Scripture says, "He bindeth the streams that they trickle not, and brings forth the thing hid to light" (Job 28:11). Things concealed from men Rabbi Akiba brings forth to light.'[27]

The two men differed in economic status as well, and a few disagreements may be traced to a difference in perspective. In the face of the internal dialectic of scriptural exegesis, it is difficult to construct a comprehensive economic interpretation of their difference, however. For example, Rabbi Tarfon held a more liberal view of the manumission of slaves than Rabbi Akiba. If the master of a servant destroys any limb, the slave may be freed without a deed of emancipation, according to Rabbi Tarfon. Rabbi Akiba holds that a deed of emancipation must be first obtained. Shall it be said here that Rabbi Tarfon, an enlightened patrician, wishes to ease the plight of injured slaves, while Rabbi Akiba expresses the ancient plebeian hostility toward the institution of slavery, the one by facilitating manumission, the other by obstructing it? This would not be unreasonable, were it not written in the Torah (Exodus 21:26): 'If a man smite the eye of his servant or the eye of his maid that it perish, he shall let him go free for his eye's sake; and if he smite out his manservant's tooth . . . he shall let him go free for his tooth's sake.' Rabbi Tarfon interprets *tooth* or *eye* to be the Biblical idiom for all limbs, while Rabbi Akiba interprets the terms more literally: while a man may indeed go free for the loss of any limb, the Torah specifies only tooth or eye, and therefore for other limbs a deed of emancipation is needed to secure and confirm freedom. Here the dialectic of exegesis is apparently at issue.[28]

Reference to the economic antecedents of the two teachers may shed light on the issue at hand in one case. Rabbi Tarfon, a country squire, was not unused to some kind of luxury while Rabbi Akiba, who had risen from poverty, had little patience with those who would lighten the yoke of the Torah. A certain man named Diskos, at Yavneh, built himself a private *mikveh* (ritual bath). When the pool was found to contain less than the required quantity of water, the question arose: what is the state of the objects purified in the pool up to that time? Rabbi Tarfon argued that the pool is regarded as acceptable until found wanting, and Rabbi

Akiba argued that every object dipped in the pool was unclean, as if it had never been dipped.[29]

Rabbi Akiba argued in Rabbi Tarfon's behalf. Once, for instance, Rabbi Tarfon made an error in declaring the law. A man brought to him an Alexandrian cow; these cows were world-renowned, and it was said of them 'Neither cow or sow leaves Egyptian Alexandria until its womb is cut out' [so that it could not breed]. Rabbi Tarfon declared the animal unfit for human consumption under the law prohibiting an animal from which a limb had been chopped off. The man threw the cow to the dogs; and later inquired of the sages at Yavneh, who advised him that the animal could have been eaten since it is explicitly taught that an animal whose womb is cut out may be eaten.

Rabbi Tarfon exclaimed, 'There goes your ass, Tarfon!' for he thought that he would have to sell an ass to compensate for the cow.

Rabbi Akiba reminded him: 'You are absolved of all costs, for you are an expert in judgment, and whoever is a recognized expert is absolved from reparation.'[30]

On another occasion, Rabbi Tarfon was refuted by a student, Judah ben Nehemiah. Judah's face brightened with joy, whereupon Rabbi Akiba turned to him and said: 'Judah, your face has lit up because you have refuted the sage. I wonder whether you will live long!' The student passed away a few months later.[31]

In one area of the law, the two teachers differ in a wholly explicable pattern. In the area of laws on the priesthood and Temple service, Rabbi Akiba stands for humanity as a factor in law, while Rabbi Tarfon seeks to establish the full measure of priestly advantage granted by tradition, law, and logic. The reason is not far to be found: Rabbi Tarfon was a priest.

Rabbi Tarfon's life-long concern for the priesthood, the Temple rites and dues, hovered in unreality, for the Temple had been destroyed in his youth, and most of the proper and necessary functions of the priesthood could no longer be performed. But maintenance of the priestly tradition had a larger meaning for Rabbi Tarfon and his generation. It meant that a link persisted between the age when Jews lived without the Temple and in exile, and the age when the Temple would once again stand as a bond between Israel and God. If the hope for the rebuilding of the Temple was to be sustained as a symbol of the messianic faith, then the continued study and practice, so far as possible, of priestly functions were assurance that the Jews kept the hope for coming redemption.

Rabbi Tarfon therefore continued to collect and consume the priestly offerings, and considered the act of eating the offerings the equivalent of the service of his forefathers in the Temple. It was told that he would eat the offerings in the morning and say, 'So have I offered the morning perpetual-offering,' and that he would do the same at twilight.[32] Once he tarried in coming to the academy, and Rabban Gamaliel questioned him. 'I was making an offering,' he explained.

'All your words are nought but foolishness! Is there any sacrifice nowadays?'

'Behold,' Rabbi Tarfon answered, 'The Scripture says, "I give you the priesthood as a gift" (Numbers 18:7). The gift refers to the priestly dues, therefore even including the heave-offerings. Thus eating the heave-offerings in the whole of the land of Israel is made equivalent to offering the sanctified offerings in the Temple itself,'[33] for both are part of the gift to the priests.

Rabbi Tarfon's priestly career began in childhood, when he went up to the Temple at Jerusalem with his uncle. During the chanting of the three-fold blessing, he strained his ears to hear the manner in which God's Ineffable Name was pronounced, but, as he reported, 'The High Priest muffled it in the midst of the chanting.' When he came of age, he did hear the Name and fell upon his face in awe, as those nearby shouted, 'Blessed be the Name of His glorious kingdom for ever and ever.'[34]

Later in his life, he recalled a Temple service, and taught

from this memory that a priest might stand in the Temple court and blast on a trumpet even though he might be lame. Rabbi Akiba contradicted him, and showed from Scripture that only priests who are without physical blemish might do so. Rabbi Tarfon answered impatiently: 'O Akiba, how long will you rake up words to bring against us! This is unbearable! May I bury my children if I did not see my Uncle Simon, the lame one, standing in the court of the Temple and blasting on his trumpet!'

'Perhaps,' Rabbi Akiba answered, 'this was on Rosh Hashanah or on Yom Kippur or on the Jubilee that you saw it?' (On these days even priests who were physically blemished might participate in the service).

'By the Temple service, you have not erred! Happy are you, O Abraham our father, that there has come from thy loins such as Akiba! Tarfon saw and forgot, Akiba reasons and conciliates memory with law! All who part from you, Akiba, part from life itself!'[35]

There were times when the two men argued at great length concerning the privileges and prerogatives of the priesthood. Rabbi Akiba was not so sympathetic to these claims; many of the priests were wealthy and Rabbi Akiba opposed what he considered the extravagance of their claims. For example, the priest may claim the first-born male of an animal. What happens if an ewe who had never before given birth bore two males and both heads came forth simultaneously? Rabbi Tarfon rules: The priest chooses the better animal. Rabbi Akiba taught: We compromise between them. Whoever takes the fatter must pay to the other half its excess value. If one of the animals should die, Rabbi Tarfon says: the priest and the farmer divide the living animal, while Rabbi Akiba says that the priest who lays claim must produce evidence that it was his, and not the farmer's animal that lived. In a number of such cases, Rabbi Tarfon consistently maintains that the priest receives the stronger animal, while Rabbi Akiba consistently urges the claim of the layman.[36] It is not that Rabbi Akiba opposed legitimate

priestly claims, but he argued that only what was positively
bestowed on the priest by the Torah ought to be his; in areas
of doubt the layman's claim ought to be accepted. The two
men argued also concerning the rights of the destroyed
Temple, and even in such abstract cases, Rabbi Tarfon
argued the maximum claims of the sanctuary and Rabbi
Akiba favoured the lay worshipper.[37]

In one instant, it is possible to offer an economic interpretation of a ritual dispute. Rabbi Akiba taught that wine, but
not olive oil, may be offered in the Temple as a freewill
offering. Rabbi Tarfon taught that oil also is acceptable.
Why was Rabbi Akiba averse to olive oil? It has been suggested that while the vine may be cultivated in a small area,
by rich and poor alike, the olive tree required large land-
holdings for its outstretched roots. A poor man would be
impatient at the sight of a rich man's miserly gift: if a farmer
was rich enough to raise live trees, he was rich enough to
donate something more fitting to his wealth than a little olive
oil. Rabbi Tarfon on the other hand could see nothing dis-
graceful in a plain offering of olive oil. He went so far as to
teach that the only suitable oil for the Sabbath lamp was
olive oil. At this a colleague demanded: 'What then will the
men of Babylon do, who have only sesame oil? and those of
Media, who have only nut oil? and those of Alexandria, who
have only colycynth oil? and those of Cappadocia, who have
only naphtha!'[38]

Besides his studies with Rabbi Akiba, Rabbi Tarfon left
his mark on the education of other noted teachers, particularly Rabbi Judah bar Ilai and Rabbi Yosi the Galilean.

Rabbi Judah came to study with Rabbi Tarfon when he
was a child, and enjoyed the patronage of the older man.
When he matured, he himself became a prominent teacher
and judge, and cited Rabbi Tarfon's precedents very frequently, and the law-in-action that he had witnessed at his
home and court. When someone asked whether it was a good
thing to have six fingers on each hand and six toes on each
foot, he reported that one such man came to Rabbi Tarfon

and he had said; 'May the like of you increase in Israel.'
Rabbi Yoi challenged this report: 'Does this really prove that
additional fingers and toes are a sign of strength? This is
what Rabbi Tarfon really said: 'May through people like
you bastards diminish in Israel.'[39]

Once Rabbi Tarfon was sitting with his colleagues and
students at the vineyard in Yavneh. Rabbi Tarfon raised a
question and answered it. 'Now', as the *Talmud* reports, 'a
certain disciple from Galilee by the name of Yosi had come
for the first time to study with the masters, and he asked
Rabbi Tarfon: "How do you know this, Rabbi?".'

Rabbi Tarfon answered, and to the amazement of all
present, Rabbi Yosi successfully refuted him. Rabbi Tarfon
kept his silence, and Rabbi Akiba lept into the argument,
introduced a third category of judgment, and settled the
dispute.

Later another question arose, on the ritual acceptability
of a certain object. Rabbi Yosi declared the object pure, and
Rabbi Akiba declared it impure. Rabbi Tarfon supported
Rabbi Yosi, and Rabbi Simon ben Nanos supported Rabbi
Akiba. Rabbi Simon bested Rabbi Tarfon, and Rabbi Yosi
bested Rabbi Simon, and Rabbi Akiba bested Rabbi Yosi.
After some time, however, Rabbi Yosi found an argument
and successfully refuted Rabbi Akiba, and the assembled
sages voted to support Rabbi Yosi's opinion.

On the day that Rabbi Yosi refuted Rabbi Akiba for the
first time, Rabbi Tarfon viewed his colleagues and commented: 'I saw the ram charging westward and northward
and southward; no beast could stand before him and there
was none who could rescue from his power; he did as he
pleased and magnified himself' (Daniel 8:4). 'This,' said
Rabbi Tarfon, 'is Rabbi Akiba'. 'As I was considering,
behold a he-goat came from the west across the face of the
whole earth, without touching the ground, and the goat had
a conspicuous horn between his eyes.' This is Rabbi Yosi the
Galiean. 'He came to the ram with the two horns, which I
had seen standing on the bank of the river, and he ran at him

in his mighty wrath. I saw him come close to the ram and he was enraged against him and struck the ram and broke his two horns.' 'The two horns,' Rabbi Tarfon continued, 'are Rabbi Akiba and Rabbi Simon ben Nanos'. 'And the ram had no power to stand before him, but he cast him down to the ground and trampled upon him.' This, again, is Rabbi Yosi. "And there was no one who could rescue the ram from his power." This refers to the thirty-two sages . . . that declared the object clean, according to the opinion of Rabbi Yosi.'[40]

In Rabbi Tarfon's day, the career of the intellect offered extraordinary satisfaction to a man of action. It was as if the slogan of society were all power to the intellectuals, for the academies ruled the body politic, legislating, judging, and determining national policy. Rabbi Tarfon spent his life in the academy as student, teacher, and judge. He was vigorous and passionate, yet through the medium of ideas and debate, he could express the full force of his personality.

Rabbi Tarfon lived in the great age of the development of Jewish law, when the cataclysmic challenge of Jerusalem's destruction brought about a brilliantly creative period in Jewish jurisprudence. The following generations continued for centuries to refine and to harmonize the great seminal ideas of these years. To list the great men of this generation, Rabbi Akiba, Ishmael, Yosi the Galilean, Judah bar Ilai, Eliezer ben Hyrcanus, Eleazar ben Azariah, Joshua ben Hananya, Rabban Gamaliel, is to list the great legislators in Jewish history.

Rabbi Tarfon joined in this work. Some speculate that he was part of the remnant of the school of Shamai, and that in the debates he fostered the views of this school of thought. Had he lived half a century earlier, this might not have been unreasonable to assume, for he was a rural squire and a priest, to whom the appeal of the Shamaites' wing of Pharaism is supposed to have been very great. But the destruction of Jerusalem weakened the Shamaites, and Rabbi Tarfon was at the time too young to have assimilated many of their teachings. He had on the other hand received some training in their traditions. In the matter of the proper stance for reciting the Shema, the earliest teaching given to a Jewish child, the school of Shamai held that the words, 'When you lie down' are to be interpreted quite literally, and that one ought to lie down. The school of Hillel held that this indicated simply the proper time to recite the Shema, that is at the time 'when you lie down', in the evening. Rabbi Tarfon nonetheless followed the teaching of the school of Shamai. He once reported: 'I was walking on the road and lay down on my side to recite the Shema (according to the teaching of the school of Shamai) and I was endangered on account of thieves.'

The sages answered: 'It served you right because you transgressed the teaching of the school of Hillel.' The later sages cited this incident to show that the words of the scribes are more precious even than the words of the Torah, for while Rabbi Tarfon was fulfilling the commandment of the Torah to read the Shema in the evening, he came into danger because he disobeyed the interpretation of the Hillelites by delaying his journey to lie down.[41]

Despite such deviation, Rabbi Tarfon rose to very great eminence in the academy at Yavneh. He conducted classes there,[42] and on a number of occasions acted as spokesman for the rabbis.[43] At Yavneh sometime after the year 80, Rabban Gamaliel succeeded to the presidency and to the great task of Rabban Yohanan ben Zakkai: to reconstruct the institutions of Jewish autonomous government after Rome's victory over Jerusalem. Rabban Gamaliel sought to prevent factionalism that would shatter the Torah into a thousand fragments. In his quest for unity and conformity to one tradition, he used the ban of heresy to enforce majority decisions, and even humiliated the most eminent teachers of the day. Some time before 95, sentiment against the vigorous rule of Rabban Gamaliel coalesced, the scholars asserted their authority and deposed the president, though for only a day.[44]

One Sabbath,[45] toward twilight, before the day that

Rabban Gamaliel was deposed, Rabbi Tarfon was sitting with his students in the shade of a dovecot. It was the end of a hot day, and a student brought the master a dipper of cold water. Rabbi Tarfon took the opportunity to teach an important law. 'What ought one to say in blessing over a cup of cold water drunk for thirst?'

'May our master teach us.'

'Blessed art Thou, O Lord our God, King of the universe, who creates living beings and satisfies their needs.'

On that day in the synagogue the Torah reading had told of the sale of Joseph into slavery, and Rabbi Tarfon began a seemingly innocent discussion of the story: 'Behold it is written, "And they lifted up their eyes and behold, a caravan of Ishmaelites came from Gilead with their camels bearing spicery, balm, and laudanum, going to carry it down to Egypt" (Genesis 37:25). Now is it the manner of Arabs to carry such things? Do they not trade in evil-smelling skins...? But God put that righteous man Joseph in the midst of pleasant odours (that he might not die of the Arabs' stench). And do we not learn from this that if in the hour of God's anger with the righteous, he has mercy on them, in the hour that he is at peace with them, how much the more will he show them mercy!' Rabbi Tarfon gave other examples of divine grace, and then turned to another part of the Torah reading, that concerning Judah. 'May I ask?'

'May our master teach us.'

'By what virtue did Judah merit the monarchy?' [Traditionally, David is descended from the tribe of Judah].

'Was it because he admitted the affair with Tamar?' (Genesis 38:26), for such an admission shows that he did not display favouritism even to himself in matters of justice, and this is a quality worthy of a king and judge.

'But,' Rabbi Tarfon answered, 'is a reward given for a sin? On what account did he *merit* the monarchy?'

'Is it because he saved his brother Joseph from death, as it is written (Genesis 37:26), "And Judah said unto his brethren, What profit is it if we slay our brother and conceal his blood? Come, let us sell him to the Ishmaelites and let not our hand be upon him, for he is our brother, our flesh!",' for such a man could appease a quarrelsome party and conciliate through compromise, and the king who can make a compromise is to be praised.

'The act of saving his brother', Rabbi Tarfon objected, 'was sufficient perhaps to atone for the act of selling him, but on what account was he worthy of the kingdom?' for even though Judah made restitution by this compromise, still it was not sufficient for the honour of majesty.

'Perhaps it was on account of his modesty, as it is written that he said to Joseph in Egypt (Genesis 44:33), "Now therefore let thy servant, I pray thee, abide instead as a bondman to my lord, and let the lad go up with his brethren. For how shall I go up to my father if the lad be not with me?" ' Thus Judah offered himself in the place of his youngest, and hence least important, brother, and a man of such modesty is certainly worthy of the throne.

Rabbi Tarfon answered: 'But was he not a pledge for his brother's safe return, and the end of a pledge is to fulfil it?' That is to say, this was not modesty, for in the first place Judah had made himself a pledge on Benjamin's safe return. 'But on what account did Judah merit the kingdom?'

'You teach us, master.'

'Because he sanctified the Name of the Holy One, blessed be He, at the Red Sea. When Israel went out from Egypt, and the tribes came to the sea, they stood there with the waters raging before them and the Egyptians pressing behind; one tribe said, I won't descend and another, I won't descend. The tribe of Judah seized the initiative and descended first, and sanctified by such faith the name of the Omnipresent. And of that hour, Scripture says (Psalms 69:2-3) "I sink in deep mire where there is no standing, I am come into deep waters where the floods overflow me. I am weary of my crying, my throat is dried, mine eyes fail while I wait for my God," and the Scripture says of Judah's courage at this hour (Psalms 114:2), "When Israel went out of Egypt, the house of Jacob from a people of strange language, Judah was His sanctuary and Israel His dominion, that is to say, Judah sanctified God's name at the sea, therefore Israel became his dominion." ' So the reason that Judah merited the monarchy was that he went so bravely to meet danger and appeared as an example to strengthen the faith of others in the Holy One, and such a man is certainly suited for dominion. And all the students agreed with Rabbi Tarfon.

Thus Rabbi Tarfon began to discourse upon a seemingly innocuous matter, and each point of his discourse became a quasi-political lecture to the regnant authority: the descendent of the House of David, the offshoot of the family tree of Hillel, must own to the qualities of leadership: fairness, ability to compromise, modesty, courage. No one could have missed the point.[46]

Despite Rabbi Tarfon's position at Yavneh, on the day that Rabban Gamaliel was desposed, he was not even considered as a successor. Rabbi Joshua, the chief of the Sanhedrin, was more eminent, but he was excluded as an immediate cause of the deposition; Rabbi Akiba did not come of distinguished parentage; so Rabbi Eleazar ben Azariah, a young man at the time, was appointed. He was descended from Ezra, and possessed the required wealth and prestige to deal successfully with the Roman authorities and the rabbis. Why for all this was Rabbi Tarfon passed over in silence? He too was wealthy, and was a priest like Rabbi Eleazar, and so claimed distinguished ancestry. It may be that his volatile temper prevented his appointment; some might think that a man with so little pity on his children that he swore by their lives would not have sufficient pity to cope with the scholars at the academy; but more probably he was not considered because by this time he had not yet attained sufficient prestige.

Later in his life, Rabbi Tarfon left Yavneh and settled on his estates in Lud (Lydda) and ruled as the rabbinic authority in that town. Lud was controlled by the foremost patrician families; sometimes, under Rabban Gamaliel, the

Sanhedrin would meet there.[47] When Rabbi Tarfon returned to Lud, he stood on the threshold of great honour. His authority waxed; he would proclaim fasts and end them; judge cases of ritual and business law, advise in all the diverse matters of rabbinic concern. On one occasion he ruled that a fraudulent sale was a sale in which the purchaser overpaid more than a third of the article's true value. At this the merchants rejoiced, since the other rabbis had permitted an overcharge of only a sixth. But Rabbi Tarfon ruled that the purchaser might return the article the whole day of the sale, rather than in the short time permitted by the rabbis. At this the merchants petitioned to revert to the rulings of the rabbis. From this incident it is clear that Rabbi Tarfon was able at Lud to contradict a ruling of the sages in his administration of the town.[48] Another time two pregnant women came before him on Yom Kippur to ask whether they might be permitted to eat. He sent to them two students, and said, 'Go and say into the ears of these women that today is Yom Kippur, and the children inside their bellies will hear and be silenced and they will not move about in their mother's bellies.' They did so to the first and the child became still, and of him they said 'Thou art he who took me from the womb. Thou didst keep me safe upon my mother's breast' (Psalms 22:9). The second did not keep still, and of him they said, 'The wicked go astray from the womb, they err from birth' (Psalms 58:3).[49]

At his court he enforced rules of testimony in opposition to established custom.[50] The rabbis taught that in the testimony given on marital matters (for example, that the husband of a woman has died and that she might remarry), it is unnecessary to test the witness' soundness, but Rabbi Tarfon did just that at his court. It once happened that a man came to give evidence on behalf of a woman that her husband had died and she might remarry. Rabbi Tarfon asked him: 'My son, what do you know concerning this woman's husband?'

'He and I were once going along the same road when a gang of robbers pursued us, and he grasped a branch of an

olive tree and pulled it down and with it forced the gang to
retreat. Lion! I said to him, I thank you. Whence did you
know, he asked, that my name was Lion? For so in fact I
am called in my own village, Johanan son of Rabbi Jonathan
the Lion of Kfar Shihaya. After some time, this same
Johanan fell ill and died.'

'Did you not tell me thus: Johanan the son of Jonathan of
Kfar Shihaya the Lion?'

'No, rabbi, no, but this is what I told you: Johanan the son
of Jonathan the Lion of Kfar Shihaya.'

'Ah yes, you have spoken well—Jonathan the son of
Johanan the Lion of Kfar Shihaya is dead.'

'No, rabbi, no, but it was Johanan the son of Jonathan the
Lion of Kfar Shihaya.' And so a few more times Rabbi
Tarfon tried to confuse the man, but he found that his
testimony was exact, and on this evidence he permitted the
wife to re-marry.[51]

In Rabbi Tarfon's time Jewish-Christians lived in Lud
(and elsewhere in the Plain of Palestine). Their numbers
were not large (it was not until the fourth century that Jewish
Palestine faced the temporal power of the Church) and the
Christianity that Rabbi Tarfon knew was little more than an
egregious heresy, not a national and religious threat.[52] He
glowed with fierce anger against the Jewish apostates, for
they had known God, he felt, and cast Him off. 'May I bury
my children if, should the writings of the apostates come into
my hands, I do not burn them and even the inscriptions of the
Ineffable Name that are in them. Should a man pursue me to
kill me and a snake run forward to bite me at once, I should
flee to a pagan temple but I should not shelter in the houses
of these, for they know and deny God, while the pagans never
knew him to deny Him. Concerning the Christians Scripture
says (Isaiah 57:8): "Behind the doors also and the posts thou
hast set up thy remembrance," that is, the remembrance of
God that was in their hands they never lost, but threw Him
behind the door. The idolaters do not recognize God, for in
idolatry they were raised and this is the faith of their fathers,

but these apostate Jews knew Him and denied Him.'[53] Rabbi
Tarfon once observed, 'I wonder whether there is anyone at
all in this generation who accepts reproof, for whenever you
say to a man, "Remove the mote from between your eyes,"
he answers back, "First remove the beam from between your
own!" '[54]

Rabbi Tarfon's career at Lud was a fitting climax to his
life: here he exercised the active authority suited to him; he
taught and judged, and here, toward the end of his life, he
apparently succeeded to the authority of Rabban Gamaliel
(after his death in 116).[55] How could it have happened that
Rabbi Tarfon should succeed Rabban Gamaliel? It was
possible because he was a priest, and because he was wealthy
and supported a number of students, two customary requirements of the *nasi*. It was possible also because Rabban
Gamaliel's son, Simon ben Gamaliel, was still a youth at his
father's death. Third, he was probably the only major scholar
who continued, by this time, to remain at Lud throughout
the year. Rabbi Eleazar ben Azariah had left the Plain for
Sepphoris in Galilee during the troubled years preceding the
revolt of Bar Kochba; Rabbi Joshua ben Hananya and Rabbi
Akiba were both deeply involved in the political crisis, the
one in negotiation with the Romans, the other proclaiming
the time for revolt. And many of the other great sages who
might have been chosen were either dead or in retirement
(Rabbi Eliezer ben Hyrcanus had settled at Caesarea, for
instance). Hence Rabbi Tarfon attained the last eminence
of the rabbinic career.

During these final years, when Rabbi Tarfon was ruling
Lud and presiding over the academy, a national assembly of
the rabbis met at the upper chamber of a house in Lud where
privacy was assured: Rabbi Akiba and the others deeply
committed to the coming struggle were present. This was to
be no scholastic argument: national policy was to be decided.
In the face of death, which should be maintained at all cost?
The study of the Torah, necessarily in semi-public assembly
and hence more dangerous, or the fulfilment of the com-

mandments and the doing of good deeds, at least partly in secret? Rabbi Tarfon said, 'Practice is greater.'

Rabbi Akiba spoke up: 'Study is greater, for it leads to practice.'

And all the scholars answered and said: 'Study is greater, for study leads to deeds.'[56]

Rabbi Tarfon lived in the memory of later generations. What was he like? When Rabbi Judah the Prince, two generations later, listed the merits of the teachers, he would say of Rabbi Tarfon: 'He was like a heap of nuts—or some say, of stones: when a person removes one from a pile, they all go tumbling over each other. This is what Rabbi Tarfon was like. When a scholar came to him and said, 'Teach me!' Rabbi Tarfon would cite for him scripture and Mishnah, Midrash, Halachah, and Agada. When the scholar departed, he went away filled with blessing and goodness.'[57]

Abba Saul once related: 'I was a grave digger and one time a cave opened under my feet and I stood in the eyeball of a corpse up to my nose. When I got out, I was told it was the eye of Absalom. And should you suggest that Abba Saul was a dwarf, Abba Saul was the tallest man in his generation, and Rabbi Tarfon reached to his shoulder, and Rabbi Tarfon was the tallest in his generation, and Rabbi Meir reached to his shoulder; Rabbi Meir was tallest in his generation, and Rabbi Judah the Prince reached to his shoulder . . .'[58]

When later generations of students envied the students of old, they would recall Rabbi Tarfon: 'Rabbi Simon ben Lakish admonished, "Do not say, how much better were the old days than these days. Do not say . . . if Rabbi Tarfon were alive, I should go to study Torah in his presence," for you only have the scholars of your own generation.'[59]

There is a tradition that he died a martyr of the Hadrianic persecutions, for his name is included, though equivocally, in a list of ten martyrs at the time of Bar Kochba.[60] After his death, his expletive, 'May I bury my children . . .' led to some curiosity as to whether his children had survived this ferocious oath (for often he was wrong). When Rabbi Judah the

Prince chanced to visit Rabbi Tarfon's town, he asked the
Lyddans, 'Has that righteous man who used to swear by the
life of his children left a son?'

'He has left no son, but a daughter's son remains, and
every harlot who is hired for two selas hires *him* for eight!'

So Rabbi Judah had the fellow brought to him and said,
'If you will repent your sin, I shall give you my daughter.'

Some say he repented; some say he married the girl and
then divorced her; others say he did not marry her at all,
lest it be said that his repentance was on her account.

And why did Rabbi Judah the Prince go to such extreme
effort to redeem Rabbi Tarfon's grandson? Because it is
taught 'He who teaches Torah to his neighbour's son will
be privileged to sit in the heavenly academy . . . .'[61]

NOTES AND REFERENCES

[1] Cf. Alexander H. Goldfahn, *Die Kirchenväter und die Agada. I. Justin
Martyr und die Agada.* Breslau 1877, 3. 'Das der Tryphon des Justin nicht
mit dem beruhmten Tanaiten R. Tarphon identisch ist, wird jetzt
allgemein anerkannt.' Cf. also T. B. Falls, Saint Justin Martyr, in L.
Schopp, Ed., *The Fathers of the Church,* N.Y. 1948, vol. VI, 12, n. 19, who
cites C. Bardenhewer, in *Geschichte der altkirchlichen Literatur,* 1913, I, 2,
p. 229, denying the historical existence of Trypho, and Th. Zahn,
'Dichtung und Wahrheit in Justins Dialog mit dem Juden Tryphon',
Zeitschrift für Kirchengeschichte, VIII (1885–1886), 37–66, affirming the
identity of Trypho with Tarfon. Since, as we shall see, Tarfon certainly
lived before the destruction of Jerusalem in 70 C.E., and in fact recalled
attending the Temple services during the priestly blessing, one is led to
doubt his having survived to 150 C.E., and his having travelled at what
would have been a very advanced age to Ephesus. There is, indeed, no
evidence whatever that Tarfon left the land of Israel, or that he engaged
in reasoned controversy with Christians. For his manner of dealing with
Christians in the land of Israel, cf. below.

[2] Avot 2.20–21. Cf. Avot de Rabbi Natan, text A, Schechter edition
42b, Goldin trans. (J. Goldin, *The Fathers According to Rabbi Nathan,*
N.H. 1955), p. 115. Cf. Also Benjamin W. Helfgott, *The Doctrine of
Election in Tannaitic Literature* (N.Y. 1954), p. 73, who suggests that this
statement is a direct response to Paul's antinomian statements in
Romans 3, 7, and Galatians 3, 5.

[3] Babylonian Talmud (hereafter = TB) Shabbat 25b. Cf. also L.
Finkelstein, *The Pharisees* (N.Y. 1946), I, 14.

[4] But see Tarfon's midrash-agada in the following: Pirke de Rabbi
Eliezer ch. 25, 61a, ch. 41, 95b, ch. 10, 25b; Numbers Rabbah 9.31

(Parallels in Sifre Numbers 8, Palestinian Talmud (hereafter = TP), Sotah 3.4, and Midrash HaGadol on Numbers, ed. S. Fish, Manchester 1940, p. 262); and Mekilta of R. Simeon b. Yohai (Jerusalem 1955), Ed. Y. N. Epstein and E. Melamed, on Ex. 6, 1, P. 5, 1.12.

⁵ An example of Tarfon's pun is Mishnah Oholot 16.1, 'May I bury my sons (ekpakh) if this halakhah is not distorted (mekupakhat)', cf. also *inter alia* Midrash Tehillim on 7.13.

⁶ TB Yoma 76a. Cf. Mekilta of R. Ishmael, Lauterbach ed., II, 113, Mekilta of R. Simeon b. Yohai p. 110 1.7, and Mekilta of R. Ishmael to Vayassa IV, lines 70–74.

⁷ Esther Rabbah 6.16. Cf. also Midrash Tehillim on 106.3. For another example of Tarfon's literalness, cf. TB Niddah 13b.

⁸ TB Niddah 61a.

⁹ TB Yevamot 118b. Cf. also TB Baba Kama 103b, Tosefta Yevamot 14.2.

¹⁰ TB Nazir 32b. Cf. also TP Sanhedrin 25a; TP Nazir 5, 4, Nazir 6 2a.

¹¹ TB Ketuvot 84a, b; TP Ketuvot 9.2–3. Cf. L. Finkelstein, *Akiba* (N.Y. 1936), 280.

¹² TB Kiddushin 69a (Mishnah 3.1). Cf. also TP Kiddushin 3.13, TB Yevamot 78a. Cf. also B. Z. Bokser, *Pharisaic Judaism in Transition* (N.Y. 1935) 108.

¹³ Cf. for example TB Yevamot 118a, b. (Mishnah 15. 6–7).

¹⁴ ARN a ch. 3, Schechter ed. p. 8b, ARN b 20a, Goldin p. 28. But see Schechter's note *ad loc.*

¹⁵ Genesis Rabbah 91.9.

¹⁶ TB Zevahim 62b. Cf. also W. Bacher, *Agadot Ha Tannaim* (Berlin 1922), II, 86.

¹⁷ Leviticus Rabbah 34.16. Cf. also Pesikta Rabbati 125. Compare Mesekhet Kallah (ed. M. Higger, N.Y. 1936), ch. 1, p. 21, and Mesekhet Kallah Rabbati, ed. M. Higger ch. 2, p. 209.

¹⁸ TB Bezah 27b (Mishnah 3.5). For other indications of his modesty, cf. TB Nedarim 62a, TP Shevi-it 4.2. For the later comment, cf. TP Bezah 3.6.

¹⁹ ARN a ch. 41, Schechter 67a, Goldin p. 173.

²⁰ TB Ketuvot 72a.

²¹ Tosefta Ketuvot 5.1. Cf. also TP Yevamot 4.12. Compare Bacher, *Agadot*, I, ii, 81, n.5.

²² TB Kiddushin 31 b, TP Pesahim, 1.1, TP Kiddushin 1.7.

²³ TP Pesahim 10.1. Cf. also M. Jastrow, *Dictionary of Talmud Babli etc.* N.Y. 1950, II, 1270.

²⁴ TB Sanhedrin 101a. Cf. also Sifre Deut. 32, Mekilta de R. Ishmael, Lauterbach ed., II, 280, Bahodesh X, 1.60–61.

²⁵ TB Shabbat 16b, 17a. Cf. Oholot 16a.

²⁶ Tosefta Oholot 15.12, cf. also TB Zevahim 13a.

²⁷ ARN a ch. 6, Schechter 15a, Goldin 42.

²⁸ TB Kiddushin 24b. Cf. TB Gittin 42b.

²⁹ TB Kiddushin 66b, cf. also Terumot 8.1, Tosefta Mikvaot 1.17. 1.18, 1.19. Cf. Finkelstein, *Akiba*, 109.

[30] TB Bekhorot 28b, cf. also TB Sanhedrin 33a.

[31] TB Menahot 68b. Cf. the text in Sifre Numbers 18, however.

[32] Sifre Zuta 293.

[33] TB Pesahim 72b, cf. also Sifre Numbers 116. Compare J. Derenbourg, *Essai sur l'histoire et la geographie de la Palestine* (Paris 1867), 377.

[34] Kohelet Rabbah 3.11. Cf. also TB Kiddushin 71a, TP Yoma, 3.7.

[35] Sifre Numbers 75, TP Yoma 1.1, TP Megillot 1.17, Tosefta Sotah 7.16, TP Horayot 3.2. Cf. also Finkelstein, *Akiba*, 82.

[36] Cf. TB Bekhorot 17a–18b.

[37] Cf. for example Terumot 7.1, TP Terumot 9.1–2.

[38] TB Shabbat 24b, TP Shabbat 2.2. Cf. Finkelstein, *Akiba*, 85–86. Compare TB Menahot 104b (Mishnah 12.5), Zevahim 91a, Sifra Vayikro 8.7, Tosefta Menahot 12.10.

[39] TB Bekhorot 45b, Tosefta Bekhorot 5.7. Cf. also TB Megillah 20a, TP Megillah 2.5, TB Nedarim 49b. Tarfon also taught Haninah ben Gamaliel, cf. TB Niddah 62a. Kiddushin 81b. Cf. also TP Sotah 2.2, Tosefta Nagaim 8.2, TB Nedarim 52a, b. (Mishnah 6.6.), Kiddushin 14a, Tosefta Yevamot 12.15, Yevamot 101 b, Sifre Deut. 291, Nedarim 19b, Niddah 38a, TP Kiddushin 3.13, Tosefta Mikvaot 7.3, TP Baba Meziah 2.8, Sheviit 5.2, Tosefta Shevi'it 4.4, for other references of Judah bar Ilai to Tarfon. Tarfon is also quoted by Rabbi Oshaiah son of Judah the Spice-dealer in TB Hullin 55b, Tosefta Hullin 3.7; and by Eliezer in Tosefta Parah 11.5.

[40] Sifre Numbers 118. Cf. TB Zevahim 57a. Cf. also Finkelstein, *Akiba*, 165. Tosefta Mikvaot 7.11, Sifre Numbers 124.

[41] Mishnah Berakhot 1.3. TB Berakhot 10b, TP Berakhot 1.4. Cf. TP Sanhedrin 11.4. But Tarfon apparently studied with Yohanan ben Zakkai, cf. TB Pesahim 72b. Cf. also L. Ginzberg, *Perushim veHiddushim baYerushalmi* (N.Y. 1900) I, 150. Cf. also J. H. Weiss, *Dor Dor veDorshav*, Vilna 1904, II, 72, and TB Yevamot 15a, TP Yevamot 1.6, Tosefta Yevamot 1.10. Also compare Mishnah Maaser Sheni 2.9, Eduyot 1.10.

[42] Cf. TB Zevahim 57a, Sifre Numbers 118, TP Yoma 1.1, TP Yevamot 4.12, D. H. Hoffman ed., Midrash Tannaim (Berlin 1909), p. 88 line 18, on Deut. 16. 19-21.

[43] TB Gittin 83a, Toma 76a, Yadaim 4.3. Sanhedrin 101a, Sifre Deut. 32, Mekilta de R. Ishmael, Lauterbach ed., II, 280; TB Gittin 9.1, *inter alia*.

[44] TB Berakhot 27b–28a.

[45] Tosefta Berakhot 4.16–17. The historical interpretation of this midrash was suggested to me by Professor Saul Lieberman of the Jewish Theological Seminary of America. The interpolated comments on the royal virtues are drawn from S. Lieberman, *Tosefta KiFshuta* (N.Y. 1955), I, 69–71. For other texts, cf. Midrash Tehillim on 76.2, Mekilta de R. Ishmael, Lauterbach ed., I, 234 (Beshallah 6.44); Mekilta of R. Simeon bar Yohai, Epstein-Melamed ed., p. 63, 1.2. Cf. also Finkelstein, *Akiba*, 231, for another interpretation. The blessing over water is taught in Mishnah Berakhot 6.8, cf. TB Berakhot 44a; Eruvin 14b, TP Berakhot 6.8.

46 For another discussion 'on that day' in which Tarfon participated cf. Yadaim 4.3, TB Berakhot 28a; cf. also Shevi-it 6.1.

47 Cf. G. Allon, *Toldot HaYehudim be-Eretz Yisrael betekufat HaMishnah veHaTalmud* (Tel Aviv 1954) I, 301.

48 Cf. *inter alia*, TB Taanit 19a, TP Taanit 3.11, TB Baba Meziah 49b, 50a, Sifra Behar 3.5, TP Baba Meziah 4.3, Weiss, *Dor*, II. 90.

49 TP Yoma 8.4.

50 Cf. TB Baba Kama 90b, Rosh Hashanah 26a. Cf. also Makkot 1.10 (TB Makkot 7a).

51 TB Yevamot 122b. Tosefta Yevamot 14.10.

52 Cf. M. Avi-Yonah, *Biyemei Roma u-Byzantion* (Jerusalem, 1952) 91–2.

53 TB Shabbat 116a, Tosefta Shabbat 14.5. Compare TB Gittin 88b.

54 TB Arekhin 16b. Cf. also Sifra Kiddushin 4.9, Sifre Numbers 1. Cf. also Derenbroug, *Essai*, 379.

55 Cf. Allon, *Toldot*, 294; Derenbourg, *Essai*, 380–382; Avi-Yonah, *Milhemet Bar Kokba* (Jerusalem 1952), 79. Allon bases his assertion on the use of the title 'Avihem shel kol Yisrael' in reference to Tarfon, in TP Megillah 1.12, Yevamot 4.14, and Yoma 1.1; he holds that this title was reserved for the *nasi*.

56 Cf. Sifre Deut. 41, TB Kiddushin 40b, Mekilta of R. Simeon bar Yohai, Epstein-Melamed ed., p. 19, 1.17; TP Pesahim 3.7; Hagigah 1.7; Shir HaShirim Rabbah 2.14; Hoffman, Midrash Tannaim, p. 34, 1.7. Weiss, *Dor*, II, 123, Finkelstein, *Akiba*, 259–261, and many others suggest that the question is, as interpreted here, how to meet the growing persecutions. Allon *Toldot*, 3124 holds, however, that the question was not how to meet the oppressive decrees, but rather, what is the chief responsibility of the sages themselves—to learning or to action?

57 ARN a ch. 18, Schechter 34a, Goldin pp. 90. Cf. also Gittin 67a.

58 TB Niddah 24b.

59 Midrash Samuel, ed. S. Buber, on 16.2.

60 Lamentations Rabbati on Lam. II, 2, para. 4.

VII

AN ARISTOCRAT OF THE INTELLECT

Rabbi Ishmael the Son of Rabbi Yosi

HEIRS OF THE Hebrew Bible, the Tannaim (religious teachers), who lived in Jewish Palestine during the first centuries of the common era, established for all time those forms of religious life and thought known as Judaism. For six generations, from before the destruction of the Temple in 70 until after the redaction of the Mishnah in 220, the Tannaim laboured to create what became the constitution for the inner life of Israel.

Although they are called rabbis, the Tannaim are not ancestors of the institution known today as the rabbinate. They were neither curates nor pastors, neither teachers in the academic sense, nor, for the most part, preachers. They did not bury or marry or officiate in religious ceremony and prayer except as part of the whole community of Israel. They were the intellectuals of a society governed by intellectuals; they governed Jewish Palestine and their legacy of law and ethics governs all of Jewish history.

Intellectualism for them was not a matter of detached speculation on problems conventionally reserved for the academy, for the philosopher. There were among them, to be sure, philosophers, as well as historians, literary critics, astronomers, physicians, logicians. But these were not the subjects of their labour, but rather the unformed matter in which to find insight into the laws that govern the larger concern of man: his subtle, ever-changing, infinitely quiet relation to God, man, and self.

R. Ishmael the son of R. Yosi lived in the sixth and last generation of Tannaim (190–220 C.E.), a generation whose conscious recognition of the passing of an old order of life recalls the mood of autumnal Europe, 1914. R. Ishmael's generation knew that it had come to the end of something very great. It ascribed to the preceding generations extraordinary sanctity; those who preceded had not only set down incontrovertible precedent in matters of law; they achieved, too, an extraordinary eminence among men for wisdom, piety, greatness. 'If they were gold, then we are dust,' R. Ishmael observed.[1] The task of this final generation, dwarfed descendants of giants, was to record, preserve, and administer the overwhelming legacy of the past. Others might indeed follow—as they did—to take up the challenge of the law to life, and of life to revelation. For the Tannaim of the sixth generation, that challenge had already been met and mastered.

While it is not an easy matter to be the last in a series of great generations, it is still less easy to be the son of one of the greatest men of the past.

R. Ishmael's father, R. Yosi the son of R. Halafta, left him a vast legacy of the intellect: the learning and teaching of a lifetime. This was riches and power in such an age, for the teaching of the past, in thought and in deed, comprehended a mandate for the present and an imperative to the future. A son of great wealth has a conventional alternative: to be profligate or to be ever penitent for paternal success. He may squander his inheritance, if of money by wasting it, and if of wisdom by forgetting it; or he may use it well and wisely. R. Ishmael accepted his inheritance, learning well what his father had to teach, and transmitted it, with what he had to add to it, to his own generation. For this he became a man of patient good humour and good sense, and his charm and wit penetrate the veil of history.

While the Tannaim lived their lives in the shadow of God's Book, R. Ishmael and his family held a particularly intimate nexus in the process of Biblical tradition, for his family claimed descent, according to ancient report,[2] from a biblical figure, Jonadab the son of Rechab. Among the refugees from Nebuchadnezzar who crowded into Jerusalem in the year 587 B.C.E., the prophet Jeremiah discovered the clan descended from Jonadab, loyally keeping the vows to dwell in tents and to abstain from wine to which Jonadab had sworn them. He cited this ancient and pious family to Jerusalem: 'Thus says the Lord of hosts . . . Will you not receive instruction and listen to my words? The command which Jonadab the son of Rechab gave to his sons . . . has been kept . . . but I have spoken to you, and you have not listened to me . . . Because you have obeyed the command of Jonadab your father and kept all his precepts and done all that he commanded you . . . therefore Jonadab the son of Rechab shall never lack a man to stand before Me.' (Jeremiah 35:12-19.)

In his generation, that man was R. Halafta.

And in his, R. Yosi the son of R. Halafta.

And in his, R. Ishmael the son of R. Yosi.

Perched on a Galilean hilltop, the city of Sepphoris (in Hebrew, Tsipori, meaning possibly 'bird-like'), the municipality whose Jewry was governed by R. Ishmael, sheltered the small brood of men who comprised the autonomous government of Palestine Jewry at the turn of the third century. Once exclusively Jewish and zealously nationalist, the city had recovered from its enthusiasms in an unforgotten and bloody devastation at the hands of Herodian armies two centuries earlier. When Herod Antipas rebuilt Sepphoris into the imposing capital of the Galilee, he wisely peopled it with both Hellenes and Jews, and the divided city kept uneasy truce during subsequent Jewish rebellions.

The profit of two centuries of peace and submission to the authorities at Jerusalem, first Jewish and then Roman, was economic and political dominion over extensive lands in northern Palestine. From Acre on the Mediterranean to Tiberias in the east, from Legion in the south to the upper reaches of the Galilee, Sepphoris dispensed justice and its Roman legions kept order. For its loyalty to the Romans in the revolt of Bar Kochba (132–135 C.E.) the city was given the title, 'Diocaesaria, Holy City of Antoninus, City of Refuge, Faithful, Beloved, Covenanted with the Holy Roman Senate and People,' an honour as welcome to the Jews as the Roman Temple, theatre, and permanent garrison which it received at the same time.

Today Sepphoris is a muddy country lane surrounded by baked mud huts, but in the days of R. Ishmael the city was the emporium of the north. With its vast lands and power, it became the most likely site for the re-establishment of the academies of Jewish self-government after the destruction of the Jewry of the plain and the south at the time of Bar Kochba. The refugee rabbis and their disciples fled to the north. They complained of the bitter mountain cold and of the closed hearts of the Sepphorean Jews, a notoriously boisterous lot. (Once a rabbi preached there on the wicked acts of the generation of the flood, depicting the clever tricks by which that generation broke into other people's homes in the dark of night. The sermon was something of a success, for that very night there were three hundred burglaries in Sepphoris.) But in this city the rabbis established what was the capital of the Jewish world for almost a century, and here they arranged the great collections of normative traditions in law and learning which are their legacy; and in Sepphoris R. Ishmael inherited and exercised the powers of self-government that remained in the hands of the Jews.[3]

The family of R. Ishmael lived at Sepphoris at least a century and a half, and governed the Jews of the city for more than half a century.

The progenitor of the family was R. Halafta, a Tanna who lived at the city at the end of the first century. Sepphoris was then a backwater of Palestinian Jewry; the great decisions were being made at Yavneh, in the plain. A provincial authority, he participated with another Galilean rabbi in the arrangement of certain prayers for fast-days, and conducted a minor academy in the city; but he sent his son R. Yosi to the south, the centre of real learning and power.[4]

R. Yosi, the son of R. Halafta, was born at Sepphoris, and after studying with his father in his early years, he went to Yavneh to study with the saintly R. Akiba. He was ordained with several others in violation of the harsh edicts of the emperor Hadrian, who aimed to pacify Palestine by destroying Jewish national autonomy in law and religion. R. Akiba was martyred, and R. Yosi fled to Asia minor. At the death of Hadrian and the abrogation of his decrees (ca. 145 C.E.) he returned to participate in the reconstruction of Jewish life; the rabbis had reassembled in the north, first at Usha, where R. Yosi joined them, and later at Sepphoris. R. Yosi found in Sepphoris a decayed and decadent Jewry, long divorced from the main currents of Jewish national life and thought.

At Sepphoris R. Yosi assumed his father's authority, building a flourishing academy. He opposed controversy and advocated a compromise between contending legal opinions. Systematically he arranged the laws and traditions of the Jews (he is credited with the only self-consciously historical work of the period), and he conducted the city's Jewish affairs with humility and good sense. He taught that it is the man that honours the office, not the office that honours the man. He knew full well what he was saying: he earned his living by tanning hides, which was equivalent in the ancient city to collecting garbage (hides were tanned with the excrement of dogs, among other things). In the teachings of the sages, these words are quoted in his name: 'Whoever honours the Torah will himself be honoured by men.' Others said of him, 'Would you fulfil the commandment, "Justice, justice shalt thou pursue!"? Then study with R. Yosi in Sepphoris.'[5]

R. Yosi's oldest son,[6] R. Ishmael, honoured his father through the ultimate flattery; life-long imitation. For instance, R. Yosi was extraordinarily chaste; R. Ishmael taught, 'So long as Israel abandon themselves to unchastity, the Divine Presence withdraws from their midst.'

R. Ishmael might have achieved greatness and power—even by the standard of his generation—had he never quoted his father. Instead he chose to begin life where his father left off, and to add to his legacy only where the inheritance did not suffice. Could he help himself if his father's wisdom surfeited two generations, his own and his son's? A link in a magnificent chain of breeding for religious life, R. Ishmael felt certain that given good luck and a fair application of the laws of genetics, as he had received, and preserved, and handed on this intangible legacy, so would others, of his family or some other, receive, and preserve, and hand down until the last moment of time what had begun with the words 'we shall do and we shall hearken.'

While R. Yosi never quoted his eldest son, R. Ishmael quoted his father hundreds of times. He loved to tell his father's teachings, and when he fell ill, the Patriarch R. Judah, his good friend, sent to cheer him up, 'Why don't you tell us some of the teachings you have told us in your father's name?' which he did, and he was cheered. R. Ishmael spoke far more often in his father's name than in his own; he taught his father's words to his students; he reported his father's tales; in all of rabbinic record, he differed with his father only once; and later generations confuse him, not without reason, with his father. One might suspect that R. Ishmael himself had no capacity to participate in complex and subtle legal discussions except on the strength of his father's great name, but actually the legal teachings of R. Ishmael, few as they are, reveal very real skill in such matters. He began, as noted, where his father left off, which was on the very frontier of legal and literary speculation; his generation, and he with it, went very little further.[7]

Scion of the ruling family in Jewish Palestine, R. Judah

the Patriarch was a close friend of R. Ishmael. He had studied with R. Yosi; his father, R. Simon the son of Gamaliel, II, had founded the academy at Usha to which R. Yosi returned from exile; and the two men were life-long friends. R. Judah felt special reverence for R. Yosi, and once remarked, 'We poor men undertake to attack R. Yosi, although our generation compares with his as the profane to the holy.' When he became patriarch at the death of his father, R. Judah established the seat of the patriarchate and regnant academy at Beth Shearim, and in the last two decades of his life, he lived at Sepphoris to gain the benefit of the healthy mountain air.

R. Judah's friendship with R. Ishmael began with self-interest. R. Ishmael was the hereditary authority of Sepphoris, a powerful community and home of the patriarch, and his submission was vital to the maintenance of the quasi-voluntary system of self-government of Jewish Palestine. This friendship, however, rested also on the profound respect the patriarch held for R. Yosi. For instance, two contradictory rulings are recorded in his name on a certain law, one strict and the other lenient. A later generation harmonized the rulings by explaining that one preceded R. Ishmael's informing the patriarch of R. Yosi's teaching in the matter, and the other followed it. Once he heard R. Ishmael's teaching in his father's name, and exclaimed, 'The elder (R. Yosi) has already ruled in the matter (and I accept his judgment).' A later teacher noted, 'Behold how the great men of this generation loved one another, for if R. Yosi had been alive, he would have sat submissively before R. Judah (although he was R. Judah's teacher, R. Judah *was* the patriarch), and although his son, R. Ishmael, who fills his father's place, does sit submissively before Rabbi, yet Rabbi accepts the ruling of the elder.'

While the friendship between the two men may well have begun in R. Judah's cultivation of those who might best carry out his programme for Jewish Palestine, the relationship deepened to affection and genuine concern out of the experience of common study of the Torah, which R. Judah shared with his intimate friends. Out of the intellectual encounter of these highly-trained minds in common problems came profound mutual respect, a sense for the partnership in a common quest of knowledge which is the prerequisite of true communication.

There was, indeed, constant interchange of ideas and information between the two men. The later sources actually confuse them and their opinions; they argue and differ; they learn from one another's words and deeds; and just as R. Ishmael asked information of R. Judah, so R. Judah asked information of R. Ishmael, not only concerning his father's teachings but concerning his own opinions as well. For example, R. Judah inquired, 'Is it permitted to take long, proud steps on the Sabbath?'

'And is it permitted on weekdays?' R. Ishmael answered. 'I maintain that long strides take away one five-hundredths of a man's eyesight, and it is only restored to him by the evening Sanctification of Wine on the Sabbath.'

'For what,' asked R. Judah, 'do the wealthy men of Palestine merit their wealth?'

'Because they give tithes, as it is said (Dt. 14:22), 'If you give tithes, then you will grow rich' (the Hebrew 'aser titaser' is punned by R. Ishmael to 'aser titasher', tithe and you will grow rich).

'And for what do the wealthy men of Babylon merit their wealth?'

'Because they honour the Torah and its students.'

'And for what do the wealthy men of other lands merit their wealth?'

'Because they keep and honour the Sabbath day.'

Besides his friendship with R. Judah, R. Ishmael enjoyed the friendship of several others, teachers, colleagues, and students. He was as proud of the honour of his students as he was of his own honour. He instructed them at any opportunity. Once when he was in Jerusalem, he noticed one of his students trembling violently. He said to him,

'You are a sinner, for it is written, "In Zion the sinners are afraid"' (Isaiah 33:14).

'But,' the student replied, 'it is also written, "Happy is the man that feareth always"' (Proverbs 28:14).

'That verse refers to words of Torah. A man ought always to be afraid lest he forget his learning.'

With his colleagues he followed the rule of strict consistency. At a consistory in the south, he abstained from voting on a question in which he had previously cast a ballot, saying, 'After having declared clean something which has been hitherto reckoned unclean, shall I now do the same in . . . another matter? I fear lest the Highest Tribunal break my skull into pieces!'[8]

R. Ishmael was very fat, and when he and his remote colleague R. Eleazar b. Simon stood belly to belly, you could drive a cart and horse between them and not touch, someone said. A certain matron once remarked, 'Your children couldn't possibly be your own,' to which he and R. Eleazar replied, 'Oh, but our wives' stomachs are even bigger than our own.'

'All the more so,' she retorted.

(Some say they answered her, 'As is a man, so is his strength,' and some say they answered, 'But Madam, love overcomes the flesh.' But, it was asked later on, ought they to have answered at all, seeing that it is written, 'Answer not a fool according to his folly, lest you be like him yourself' (Proverbs 26:4). But, it was answered, they did not want her to bring suspicion on their children.)

His corpulence caused him more than a little trouble, and it was well that he could bear it lightly. Once two students, R. Hiyya and R. Simon, the son of R. Judah the Patriarch, were sitting and discussing prayer. One remarked, 'He who prays ought to direct his eyes downward, as it is said, "And my eyes and my heart were there all the days"' (I Kings 9:3), and one said, 'He should direct his eyes upward, as it is said, "Raise up your hearts . . ."' (Lam. 3:41).

While they were talking, R. Ishmael happened along and asked what they were talking about.

'Praying,' they answered.

'This is what father taught, "He who prays ought to direct his eyes downward and his heart upward, to fulfil these two Scriptures".'

In the meantime R. Judah came along to the academy. The two students, being light and nimble, quickly took their places, while R. Ishmael could only move to his place with slow, clumsy plodding. Abba Judah, the student prefect, exclaimed, 'And who is this who treads over the heads of the holy people?' for all the students had taken their places on the ground around the teacher, while R. Ishmael still stood.

'It is I, Ishmael, the son of R. Yosi, for I have come to study Torah with Rabbi.'

'And are you fit to study Torah with Rabbi?'

'And was Moses fit to study Torah from the mouth of God?'

'And are you Moses?'

'And is your master God?'

R. Ishmael bore the mark of the well-born: arbitrariness and contrariety. Once he met a man loaded with faggots as he was walking along the road. The man stopped, put down his load, rested, and then turned to R. Ishmael, 'Help me take them up!'

'And how much are they worth?'

'Half a zuz.'

R. Ishmael gave the man half a zuz, and declared the faggots free and ownerless property, thinking that if another were to happen along, he might take them and not be guilty of misappropriating the property of another.

The man went back and declared his possession of the now ownerless property. R. Ishmael thereupon gave him another half-zuz and declared the bundle free to all the world. The man made a gesture toward the bundle, to reacquire it. R. Ishmael then said, 'To all the world, these faggots are a gift, but to you they remain my property.'

R. Ishmael was by nature kind and undisputative. He provided food for a woman whose husband had deserted her; in arguments among the rabbis he would offer compromise between uncompromising disputants. As it happened, his compromise was rejected out of hand by both sides.

Above all, he was unwavering in honesty. He lived by the honesty of the noble and well-born: to live otherwise is unthinkable. He had a tenant who made it a practice to bring him his share of the produce on a fixed weekday. One week he came a few days in advance, at which R. Ishmael inquired, 'What is the difference, that you come earlier this week?'

'I have a case to be tried, and I thought that I'd bring the master his produce on the way.'

At this R. Ishmael refused to accept the basket, and declared himself unfit to judge any case in which the tenant was a party. He commented on this incident, 'Woe unto those who take bribes. For behold, I was suspect of favouring a tenant from whom I received but my own goods—how much the more so would a judge be swayed even by the most innocent bribe!'

Recalling this incident, a later generation commented, ' ". . . and who has not taken a bribe concerning the innocent" (Ps. 15:15)—this is R. Ishmael, who would not even take what was his own!'[9]

It was well for his generation that R. Ishmael was scrupulously honest, for in inheriting his father's position in Sepphoris, he became magistrate of Sepphoris Jewry. Even when judging in his own right, he was never free of his father's influence, for even a humble woman reminded him in court, 'This is what I heard from your father: "Whenever it is possible to judge leniently in such a matter, one does so . . ." ' He himself almost always followed his father's precedents.

His freedom of decision was limited not only by his father's precedents, but also by the presence in the city of the patriarch and his academy. Before R. Judah came to Sepphoris, R. Ishmael judged a case contrary to the patriarch's opinion, for which R. Judah criticized him; but after his coming, about the year 200, R. Ishmael accepted his authority without apparent question or complaint. In his care for scrupulously honest juridical procedure, R. Ishmael warned, 'Never judge alone, for none judges alone but One.' He consistently bespoke the participation of other judges, and taught, 'Do not say to your fellow judges, "Accept my opinion," for only the majority, and not the individual, have such a right.'

He bore a heavy burden of justice and kept court for a busy city. This was the substance of his career, and he was a humane and intelligent judge. He judged cases touching every aspect of Jewish life: ritual, commercial, social. He legislated in favour of slaves, of slandered virgins; judged matters relating to the Sabbath, female purity, ritual cleanliness, property rights. He unknotted snarled questions such as this: 'If a man sold a sycamore tree in the land of his neighbour, does the land accompany the tree?' R. Ishmael held that it does; his associates held it does not. He ruled that if a man broke through a new window into a courtyard on which he is a partner, he is permitted to retain it. 'You have proven stronger, for the opposing litigants did not challenge your action effectively at the start.' R. Hiyya ruled somewhat laconically, 'You have worked to open up the window, now work to stop it up.'

R. Ishmael was particularly interested to facilitate the annulment of foolish vows. He lived in a world which took very seriously the sanctity of speech, and if a person vowed in anger, he must fulfil his vow in sorrow, or seek to have the vow annulled by act of rabbinical court. The court would annul a vow if the judges could find extenuating circumstances to show that the man never really meant the vow in the first place.

In his youth, R. Ishmael made a vow, and came before the rabbis to have it annulled. The rabbis asked him, 'Did you vow with this contingency in mind?'

'Yes.'

'And with that in mind?'

'Yes.'

A number of times they asked, and he, in his simplicity, admitted that he had vowed with every conceivable extenuation in mind. Finally a gruff fuller, seeing how he troubled the rabbis, slapped him with a fuller's-basket, at which R. Ishmael exclaimed, 'I certainly did not vow to be smitten by a fuller'; and the rabbis thereupon annulled the vow.[10]

As magistrate of Sepphoris Jewry, R. Ishmael was inclined to co-operate with the Roman authorities of the town. The times were peaceful, though the Jews were not; indeed they would never fully submit to Rome's rule in their homeland, but they could not forget the disastrous results of the preceding revolts (70, 132–135) in which Jewish Palestine met calamity upon calamity. R. Ishmael determined that his years would be years of peace and prosperity for Jewish Palestine. When, for instance, a Roman general came to town, R. Ishmael permitted Jews to help provender his forces even on the Sabbath.

His co-operation extended, however, to actions which some thought treasonable. He handed Jews over to the Roman authorities. These were years in which Jewish brigands roamed the Galilean hills, the remnants of a local insurrection brought on by an imperial war of succession. It was such Jewish brigands that R. Ishmael gave up to Rome, and it is, unhappily, this action which comes first to the mind of those who remember the name of R. Ishmael, the son of R. Yosi, to this day.

Sepphoris Jewry took the side of Lucius Septimius Severus in his war against the legions of Piscennius Niger in 193–194. Niger had ruled the Levant, and had distinguished his administration by voicing regret that he could not tax the air Jews breathed. Septimius decisively defeated Niger, and in his victory burned Neapolis (Shechem, the Samaritan sanctuary) an act hardly unpopular with his Jewish allies. He followed this with harsh anti-Samaritan edicts. In his hour of triumph, however, Septimius saw his Jewish allies revolt, particularly in the neighbourhood of Sepphoris. This was not a national rebellion, and was mainly a guerilla action by youths who ignored the cautious leadership of the rabbis. But the rebels succeeded in winning the sympathy of the Jewish masses, particularly since they imparted a messianic character to their rebellion by hinting at the reconstruction of the sanctuary in Jerusalem. R. Ishmael's friend, R. Eleazar, commented on this, 'When the children advise you to build the temple, do not listen to them.' If the rabbis thought the revolt could succeed, they would have led it. Since they did not, they opposed it, led by R. Judah and his functionaries, including R. Ishmael.

It was in this situation that an old man—some say it was the prophet Elijah—met R. Ishmael walking down the road. He asked him, 'How long are you going to hand over to the slaughterer the people of God?'

'And what shall I do? It is a royal appointment which I cannot avoid.'

'Your father fled to Asia Minor. You could flee to Laodicea.'

This is a classic encounter. The zealot claims undeviating loyalty to people, land, and nation; the collaborator claims wise and supple loyalty to the best interest of people, land and nation. Like R. Judah, in whose service many rabbis co-operated with Rome, R. Ishmael held that the national interest was peaceful co-operation with the imperial power, whose dominion extended back three centuries and forward for two, whose invincible power had utterly destroyed the national sanctuary in 70 and internal government in 135. Co-operation meant at least limited self-government. To R. Ishmael and his colleagues loyalty to the nation did not demand undeviating rebellion against all things Roman. He and his colleagues, particularly R. Eleazar, who was, after all, the son of a fiery zealot of the earlier revolt, were not at all prepared to risk all that is for what might never come to pass.[11]

R. Ishmael was more than a municipal judge and magistrate. He was also a student, like his colleagues, of the Bible, the text from which law was derived. In the text of the Bible he and his colleagues found infinite wisdom. In it they immersed themselves and from it they took insight for the ages. For them the Bible was the ultimate source of information on morality, religion, and theology; but also on geography, history, wisdom. Through skilful literary criticism all this could be found out.

In the text of the Bible, R. Ishmael discovered the secret of growing old: 'When men of wisdom grow old, they gain greater wisdom, as it is said, "Wisdom is with the aged and understanding in length of days" (Job 12:12), and when men of ignorance grow old, they gain in foolishness, as it is said, "He deprives of speech those who are trusted, and takes away the discernment of the elders".'

In its text he discovered new dimensions of theology: R. Kahana taught in his name, 'What is the meaning of the verse "To the choirmaster (lam mi naatseach)" (Ps. 4:13)? Sing to Him who rejoices when he is conquered (when they conquer him, mi na-tsechim). For behold, man's attribute is not like God's attribute. When man is conquered, he is sad, but when God is conquered, he rejoices, as it is said, "Therefore He said he would destroy them, had not Moses his chosen one stood in the breach before him to turn his wrath from destroying them" (Ps. 102:23), that is, Moses was his chosen one because he turned away his anger from destroying, and he rejoiced in Moses' success.'

But the Bible was foremost a battleground for contending sects and religions, and the interpretation of Scripture was a mortal issue. The sectarians, who were numerous and abounded in Sepphoris, sought to foist on the biblical text the doctrine of plural deity. A sectarian said to R. Ishmael, 'It says (Gen. 19:24), "God rained down on Sodom and Gomorrah brimstone and fire, from the Lord, from heaven." Should it not have said "From himself"?' Perhaps the repetition of 'From the Lord' implies a second deity.

A fuller thereupon said, 'Rabbi, permit me to answer him. It says "Lamech said to his wives Ada and Zillah, Hear my voice oh wives of Lamech" (Gen. 4:23). It should have said, "My wives", but this is simply the biblical idiom.'

R. Ishmael went up to pray in Jerusalem, and on the way he passed by the Samaritan sanctuary (before its destruction in 193/194). He was accosted by a Samaritan who asked where he was going.

'To pray in Jerusalem.'

'Would it not be better to pray at this holy mountain rather than at that dunghill in Jerusalem?'

'I'll tell you what you're like: you're like a dog panting after carrion. You know idols are hidden under your mountain, as it is written, "And Jacob hid them" (Gen. 35:4), and therefore you are anxious to pray there. You are really idolaters at heart.'

'This man,' the Samaritan told his friends, 'wants to take away our idols.'

When R. Ishmael heard this, he rose up and fled into the night.[12]

NOTES AND REFERENCES

[1] Yer. Git. 6:7.

[2] Gen. R. 98:7.

[3] On Sepphoris, cf. Schuerer, E., *A History of the Jewish People in the Time of Jesus Christ*, II, i, 138–139; *Jewish Encyclopedia*, art. by S. Kraus, XI, 198–200; Buechler, A., *Social and Political Leaders of the Jewish Community of Sepphoris in the 2nd and 3rd centuries*, 4; Avi-Yonah, M., *Historical Geography of the Land of Israel* (Hebrew), 131–134; B. B. 75b; Yer. Mas. Sh., V; Sanh. 109a.

[4] For traditions taught by R. Yosi in the name of R. Halafta his father, cf. *inter alia*, Kil. 16:6; Tos. M. Sheni 1:13; Tos. B. B. 2:10; Tos. Oholot, 5:6; Bechorot 26a.

On R. Halafta, cf. arts. in *Jewish Encyclopedia*, and Margoliot, M., *Encyclopedia of the Sages of the Talmud and the Geonim* (Hebrew), I, 311.

On R. Yosi, b. R. Halafta, cf. *inter alia* Avot 4:8, Yoma 66b; Yeb. 63b; B. K. 70a; Meilah 17b; Sanh. 14a, 109a, Shabbat 33b, 48a; B. B. 75b; Yer. A.Z. 3:1; M.K. 25b. He is mentioned more than three hundred times in the Mishnah alone.

[5] On the midrash of 'Justice, justice shalt thou pursue,' cf. Sanh. 32b.

[6] On the birth record of R. Yosi's family, cf. Shabbat 118b; Ber. R. (Theodore-Allbeck p. 1039) reports that this was a levirate marriage. Cf. also Yer. Yeb. 1:1.

On R. Halafta, cf. M.K. 21a, also Midrash Tehillim (ed. Buber) 100:2.

On Simon b. Halafta (R. Ishmael's nephew), cf. Mishnah Uktzin, 3:12. Hyman proves that he is not the brother of R. Yosi and the son of R. Halafta the elder by showing his frequent contacts with the patriarch, R. Judah (Hyman, *History of the Tannaim*, III, 1174). He studied with R. Meir and was apparently friendly with the colleagues of his uncle R. Ishmael, R. Hiyya and R. Simon the son of R. Judah. But there is no recorded contact between the two men. He was very poor until the patriarch gave him a portion of food, and later R. Hiyya gave him a field (Ruth R. 5:21). Cf. also Koh. R., 3:2; B.M. 86a.

R. Menahem is quoted by his father R. Yosi b. R. Halafta in Tos. B.M. 11:3, and he quotes a discussion he had with his father in Tos. Tevul Yom 2:8. R. Yochanan says that R. Judah the patriarch quoted many *mishnayot* in R. Menahem's name without citing him by name, cf. Meg. 26a, Ket. 101b.

R. Eleazar is quoted by R. Yosi in Sifre Dt. 148, Pes. 117a, Yoma 67a. He quotes his father R. Yosi in Men. 54b, Pesikta de R. Kahana 1, 4a. For his connections with R. Simon b. Yochai, cf. Meilah 17b, Shmot R. 52: 5. W. Bacher (Dor Dorve-Dorshav, II, ii, 96–104) suggests that R. Yosi cites his son in order to give the opinion of the school of R. Ishmael, or because R. Eleazar died in his father's lifetime. Reports, in the trip to Rome, indicate that R. Eleazar taught there, cf. Tos. Niddah 7; Mikvaot 4:7, Niddah 48a.

Bacher does not identify R. Menahem with Vardimus but he suggests that R. Avtilas and R. Eurydemos b. R. Yosi are one and the same.

[7] For the statement on chastity, cf. ARN ch. 38; cf. also Num. R. 7:10, Sifre Deut. 254, 258. Buechler (op. cit.) p. 47 says that this indicates that Sepphoris was a centre of sexual laxity, but I believe the statement is better understood within the context of the family tradition. For the request of R. Yosi's teachings when R. Ishmael was sick, cf. Shabbat 15a, Pes. 118b; A.Z. 8b.

R. Ishmael quotes his father, in the following places *inter alia*.; Bavli: Yeb 67a, b; Shabbat 52a, 81a; Eruv. 28b; Pes. 32b; Pes. 103a; Taanit 30a; Sukkah 20a; Ket. 104a; Gittin 7a; Nedarim 21a, 62a; Hullin 25b; Hallah 1:4 (cf. Pes. 37b); Sukkah 18a.

Yerushalmi Maaser 1:3, Ter. 2:3; Shabbat 3:1; Shevi-it 6:1; Demai 1:1; Kilaim 1:1; Shabbat 5:1, 8:6; Pes. 2:6 (cf. Hallah 1:4, Pes. 37b); Terumot 3:1.

Tosefta Terumot 4:6, Maaser Rishon 1:1, Hallah 1:1, Shabbat 4:1, Sukkah 1:10, Taanit 4:11, Yevamot 9:1, Kelim 4:18, Niddah 4:12,

Tabarot 11:12, Cf. Allon G., *History of the Jews in Palestine in the Time of the Mishnah and the Talmud* (Hebrew) I, 77.

He taught his students what his father had taught him cf. Shab. 49a. He reports his father's deeds as a legal precedent in Yer. Berakhot 4:1, Yer. Taanit 4:1, Bavli Berakhot 27b; Genesis R. 10:2; Tos. Terumot 4:2; Yer. Terumot 2:2. He tells stories he heard from his father in Kid. 71a, Sifra 78. He differs with his father only in Yer. Ket. 1:10. He is confused with R. Yosi in Eruv. 86b. He defends his father's honour in B. M. 85b, cf. Niddah 14b.

8 R. Judah's attitude to R. Yosi is reflected in Yer. Gittin 48b, Sanh. 24a, Shab. 51a. R. Judah transmits R. Yosi's teachings in Men. 14a, but differs from him very frequently in the Mishnah. Cf. Ket. 72b.

Allon (op. cit. II, 131, 145) explains that it was to the self-interest of the patriarch to maintain good relations with his several intimates.

Tosafot Shabbat 51a, b, prove that actually R. Yosi is considered a greater figure in the law than R. Judah, citing Niddah 14b.

On creation cf. Gen. R. 10:9.

Other sources quoted are found as follows:

Niddah 14b, Yer. Kil. 9:3; Yer. Ket. 12:3, also Kid. 33a; Yer. B.M. 5:2 (cf. the commentary called Korban Adah, whose remarks I have interpolated for clarity; cf. also Yer. Meg. 4:1).

Eccl. R. 1.7.9. Eruv. 86b, 86a. Allon (op cit. II, 145) states that R. Judah was not particularly friendly towards other teachers in his generation, excepting a few favourites; Buechler (op. cit. 226) states that R. Judah commonly used colleagues of his court for official missions.

R. Judah and R. Ishmael study together, cf. Lev. R. 15; Yer. Shabbat 16:1; Lam. R. 4:20, and parallel in Yer. Shab. 16:1.

On the interchange of information and ideas, cf. *inter alia*, B.M. 73a, Yer. Orlah 2:3, Yer. Yeb. 12:4, Shabbat 113b, 119a; cf. Gen. R. 11:2 for another text.

On his interchange with R. Judah in matters of proper conduct, cf. Pes. 112b.

R. Ishmael studied with R. Judah b. Ilai, before whom he recited his father's teachings (Sukkah 18a). He taught R. Hanina b. Hama, cf. Kid. 71a, Yer. Ket. 5:8; and R. Hanina cf. Niddah 20a; R. Kahana, cf. Pes. 119a, Shabbat 15a, and R. Anani b. Sason, cf. Shabbat 64b; and R. Simon the son of R. Judah, cf. Zeb. 59a; and R. Huna, cf. Hullin 124a. All these quote his teachings.

For the incident with the student cf. Ber. 60a.

The difficult matter of the consistory in the South is thoroughly analyzed in Buechler, 188-192, and is found in the following sources, Tos. Oholot 18:18, Yer. Shev. 6:1; Yer. Shavuot 7:2.

For differences with R. Hiyya, cf. Yer. Erub, 7:1, Sanh. 29b; R. Hiyya accepts R. Ishmael's opinion, cf. Sanh. 29b.

9 For sources quoted cf. B.M. 86a, Pes. 86b; Yeb. 105b; B.M. 30b; Yer. Ket. 13:1; Pes. 20b; B.K. 116a, Hullin 137a, Ket. 105b, Makkot 24a.

10 Yer. Erub. 7:10, Babli Erub. 80b, 86b, Sukkah 16b. Yer Ket. 13:1 presents the conflicting opinion.

Yer. B.M. 5:6. For cases R. Ishmael judged, cf. above, and *inter alia* Sanh. 24a, Eccl. R. 1.7.9.

Allon (op. cit. I, 141) explains that there was a tendency for unauthorized experts to judge by themselves in matters in which they had special competence. Gulak, *Foundations of Hebrew Jurisprudence* (Hebrew) IV, 86, suggests that this was true only later in the early Amoraic period, but beside this incident, there are cases as early as in the generation of Yavneh (cf. *inter alia*. R. Tarfon's judgment, Sanh. 32a etc.). For other cases R. Ishmael judges as the regnant authority in Sepphoris, cf. *inter alia*, Shab. 64b, Pes. 20b; B.B. 59b, 109a, Sanh. 29b; Zeb. 59a; B.B. 59b; Yer. B.B. 4:8; B.B. 109a. Sifre Num. 134. For slave-law, cf. Yer. Gittin 4:4; Gittin 39a; for cases on ritual purity, cf. Yer. Oholot 5:1; Tos. Shabbat 13:17; female purity, cf. Midrash Shmuel 2:3; Niddah 20a. On the accused bride, cf. Yer. Ket. 1:1. On oaths, cf. Nedarim 23a, 66b. On interpretations of dreams cf. Ber. 56b, Yer. Maas, Sh. 4:6, Lam. R. 1.1.14. The text in Ber. states only R. Ishmael, but S. Rabinowitz *ad loc*. p. 156, Dikduke Soferim, determines the proper reading, along with the parallels, as R. Ishmael b. R. Yosi. Buechler, op. cit. 249–250, states that the questioner in the interpretation of dreams was a *Min*; cf. also Goldfahn, in *Monatschrift* 1870, XIX 69 f. who thinks he is a gnostic.

[11] On his co-operation with the Romans, cf. Yer. Erub. 8:8, B.M. 83b; Buechler, op cit , 226, explains that this was in the service of the patriarch. On conditions in Jewish Palestine at this time, cf. Allon, op. cit. I, 1337, II, 120–121. The rabbis co-operated with Rome in times of administrative leniency, but only against their will. For details of this war, cf. H. Graetz, Graetz Monatsschrift, XXXIII (1184), 481–496. On R. Eleazar cf. Tos. A. Z. 1:19. cf. especially S. Lieberman, 'Palestine in the Third and Fourth Centuries C.E.', *Jewish Quarterly Review*, n.x., xxxvi, 4, 329–370, and xxxvii, 1, 31–54; and J. Juster, *Les Juifs dans l'Empire Romain*, (Paris 1914), II, 195.

[12] Shabbat 152a, Pes. 119a, Gen. R. 26:3, Cant. R. 4.4.8. Historical speculations cf. Sifra Behar 84a; Tos. Arechin 5:16, and parallels Meg. 10a, Shavuot 16a, Arechin, 32b. Cf. also Sanh. 38b, Yer. A.Z. 5:4 Allon, op. cit., II, 116, suggests that there was a permanent settlement of Jews in Jerusalem at this time, cf. also II, 245, note 7. For other sources of R. Ishmael's attitude toward Samaritans, cf. Yer. A. Z. 2:1; Tos. A.Z. 3:4.

INDEX

INDEX TO BIBLICAL PASSAGES CITED